**English Literature**

Poetry and Anthology

Michaela Blackledge

Jane Flintoft

Andy Mort

Alison Rudd-Clarke

Series Editor

Imelda Pilgrim

 Nelson Thornes

Published in 2010 by:
Nelson Thornes Ltd
Delta Place
27 Bath Road
CHELTENHAM
GL53 7TH
United Kingdom

10 11 12 13 14 / 10 9 8 7 6 5 4 3 2 1

A catalogue record for this book is available from the British Library

ISBN 978 1 4085 0600 4

Cover photograph: Heather Gunn Photography

Page make-up by Pantek Arts Ltd, Maidstone

Printed and bound in Croatia by Zrinski

Contents

Introducing the new spec

The Anthology

There is little difference between the function of the Anthology in this specification and its role in previous ones: it is a free resource provided by AQA which can be used flexibly by teachers in conjunction with the prescribed texts.

Although teachers will find some previously anthologised poems and short stories in *Moon on the Tides*, the majority of texts are new. To facilitate planning and affordable provisions of resources, teachers value continuity, and there are a number of 'old favourites' in the set text lists in Unit 1: Exploring Modern Texts. Equally teachers are motivated by the stimulus provided by fresh material, and will welcome opportunities to explore new territory after working with an Anthology that had remained unchanged for a number of years. While most of the material is new, the place of the Anthology in the Literature course structure is not so very different.

The Anthology will be used predominantly in the Literature course, but students taking GCSE English only will have to cover Exploring Cultures in Unit 1 and the English, Welsh and Irish Literary Heritage requirements in Unit 3, and they may choose Anthology texts to write about in their controlled assessment pieces. Additionally, as has always been the case, Anthology texts will provide stimuli for Creative writing controlled assessment tasks in GCSE English/English Language, as well as for Speaking and listening assessments.

In Literature, the short stories in the Anthology have a similar purpose to their role in previous anthologies: they offer alternative prose texts to the novels and non-fiction text set in the two Unit 1 components, Modern Prose or Drama (Section A) and Exploring Cultures (Section B). As previously, all stories will need to be studied, since the whole collection of stories in a component is the equivalent of one longer text. There will be no requirement for candidates to make comparisons between stories.

Although the Anthology differs in structure from the last one, it will look not unfamiliar to teachers who have worked with earlier AQA anthologies, in that the poems are organised into (four) thematic clusters. Approximately half of the 15 poems in each cluster are contemporary, and the rest are poems by writers drawn from the English, Welsh and Irish Literary Heritage list of authors. Previously the distinction has been between contemporary and pre-1914 poets; the changed nomenclature shifts the balance of content somewhat, in that there are more poems by relatively modern deceased poets.

The choice

There are two routes that can be taken to meet the Shakespeare and the English, Welsh and Irish Literary Heritage, and the poetry requirements. Students can either:

- write about poetry in the examination and cover Shakespeare and the English (Welsh and Irish) Literary Heritage via controlled assessment (Route 1)
- write about Shakespeare and the English (Welsh and Irish) Literary Heritage in the examination and cover poetry via controlled assessment (Route 2).

The two routes are further illustrated in tabular form overleaf.

Unit 1: Exploring Modern Texts

External examination (60 marks, 40% in total):

- Section A – Modern Prose or Drama (45 mins, 30 marks)
- Section B – Exploring Cultures (45 mins, 30 marks)

Route A

Unit 2: Poetry Across Time

External examination (54 marks, 35% in total):

- Section A – Poetry cluster from the Anthology (45 mins, 36 marks)
- Section B – Responding to an unseen poem (30 mins, 18 marks)

Unit 3: The Significance of Shakespeare and the English Literary Heritage

Controlled assessment (40 marks, 25% in total)

Route B

Unit 4: Approaching Shakespeare and the English Literary Heritage

External examination (54 marks, 35% in total):

- Section A – Shakespeare (45 mins, 30 marks)
- Section B – Prose from the English Literary Heritage (30 mins, 24 marks)

Unit 5: Exploring Poetry

Controlled assessment (40 marks, 25% in total)

If teachers choose the controlled assessment poetry route (Unit 5: Exploring Poetry), study of the Anthology is not compulsory, but equally it provides a rich source of material from which to select texts in order to meet the specification requirements. An oral outcome may not be submitted for this unit.

If teachers choose the examination poetry route (Unit 2: Poetry across Time), students must study at least one Anthology cluster in its entirety, as they will have to write about a named poem chosen from the cluster in the exam. They will also be required to compare the named poem with another poem of their choice from within the cluster.

The newest and perhaps most challenging feature of the Literature specification is the requirement for students to write about an unseen poem as well as Anthology poems in the Unit 2 examination option. This is a welcome development which gives teachers the opportunity to design their own courses to equip students with an independent critical approach to reading which should be an excellent preparation for the demands of Advanced Level and Higher Education courses. While teachers will be keen to follow their own enthusiasms, poems in the three Anthology clusters not selected for specific study will provide a resource bank invaluable in preparing students for the Unseen part of the paper.

Strictly speaking, the Unseen section does not belong in a book of Anthology support materials, but it is an integral part of the book because the development of independent reading skills obviously supports the teaching of set Anthology poems and literature in general. As unseen poetry appreciation has not been a feature of AQA exams for many years, teachers might particularly appreciate guidance on this new development.

All three parts of this book and the corresponding Student Book, paired with the supporting online resources, are based on a shared philosophy that what teachers most value are suggestions for practical activities which encourage active approaches to reading and encourage independent learning, supported by detailed notes and suggestions for further reading in this Teacher's Book. The chapters of the Student Book are not intended to be worked through mechanically; teachers will wish to modify all or some of them in their specific lesson planning. However, the activities are intended to serve as 'models', exemplifying approaches which teachers are encouraged to imitate and modify using texts of their choice. In addition, the structured approaches to set Anthology texts afford students excellent support in final revision activities.

Assessment Objectives

There are four Assessment Objectives for GCSE English Literature:

AO1: respond to texts critically and imaginatively; select and evaluate relevant textual detail to illustrate and support interpretations.

AO2: explain how language, structure and form contribute to writers' presentation of ideas, themes and settings.

AO3: make comparisons and explain links between texts, evaluating writers' different ways of expressing meaning and achieving effects.

AO4: relate texts to their social, cultural and historical contexts; explain how texts have been influential and significant to self and other readers in different contexts and at different times.

The first two Assessment Objectives relating to meaning and writers' techniques are assessed in all units. AO3 is assessed only in Units 2, 3 and 5. AO4 is covered in only Units 1, 3 and 4.

Quality of Written Communication will be assessed in all Literature units, as in the previous specification.

Areas of overlap between Literature and Language

A quick look at AO3 Studying written language for GCSE English Language reveals the extent to which it overlaps with its partner subject, GCSE English Literature. The areas of overlap are highlighted below:

GCSE English Language: AO3 Studying written language

- Read and understand texts, selecting material appropriate to purpose, collating from different sources and making comparisons and cross-references as appropriate.
- Develop and sustain interpretations of writers' ideas and perspectives.
- Explain and evaluate how writers use linguistic, grammatical, structural and presentational features to achieve effects and engage and influence the reader.

This demonstrates the extent to which the skills you are developing in your students for GCSE English Literature are directly transferrable to GCSE English Language.

Introducing and using the Nelson Thornes resources

Nelson Thornes and AQA

Nelson Thornes has worked in partnership with AQA to ensure that the Student Book, the Teacher's Book and the accompanying online resources offer students and teachers the best support possible for their GCSE course. The print and online resources together **unlock blended learning**; this means that the links between the activities in the book and the activities online blend together to maximise students' understanding of a topic and help them to achieve their potential.

All AQA-endorsed resources undergo a thorough quality assurance process to ensure that their contents closely match the AQA specification. You can be confident that the content of materials branded with AQA's 'Exclusively Endorsed' logo have been written, checked and approved by AQA senior examiners, in order to achieve AQA's exclusive endorsement.

Student Book

The Student Book has been divided into three sections, each with a predominant focus on a given area, to demonstrate clear coverage of the assessment objectives and for clarity of organisation:

● Section A: Reading poetry

● Section B: Poetry from the Anthology

● Section C: Short Stories

Each section of the Student Book concludes with exam and/or controlled assessment chapters. These chapters draw together the skills developed throughout the section and show students how to apply them in their assessments.

All Student Book chapters include:

Objectives

A list of student-friendly learning objectives at the start of the chapter that contain targets linked to the requirements of the specification.

Activity

Activities to develop and reinforce the skills focus for the lesson.

Check your learning

A list of points at the end of the chapter that summarise what students have covered.

Some (but not all) chapters feature:

Biography | Background

Biographies and backgrounds provide students with additional information about a writer or a text.

Key terms

Terms students will find it useful to be able to define and understand. The definitions also appear in the glossary at the end of the Student Book.

Links

Links to other areas of the Student Book or additional resources that are relevant to a particular learning point.

Stretch yourself

Extension activities to take the work in a chapter further.

Guidance from the examiners or moderators on how to avoid common pitfalls and mistakes, and how to achieve the best marks in the exam or controlled assessment.

The texts and activities in the Student Book have been chosen by the writers to appeal to students but no single textbook or set of teacher notes can account for the wide range of young people encountered in the classroom. It is the combination of a good teacher and a good textbook that makes the latter most effective. You know your students best. Be prepared to use the materials in the Student Book selectively, to introduce your own texts and activities and to add explanation or differentiated criteria. In this way you will best suit the needs of the students who sit in front of you, and maximise the potential of the Student Book.

Teacher's Book

The Student Book provides a structured route for the development of the skills denoted by the assessment objectives. The Teacher's Book acts as a guide to the Student Book, drawing your attention to specific points of focus, providing answers to and guidance on the activities and suggesting alternative approaches and possible extension work. They are not intended to be in any way prescriptive.

Each section of the Teacher's Book follows the order of the Student Book and includes chapter-by-chapter guidance on using the Student Book resources.

In addition to the chapter-by-chapter coverage, each section also contains at the start:

- an overview of the section and the AOs
- a resources overview listing all the activities in the Student Book, along with the worksheets and interactive resources available online in **kerboodle!**

- a range of activities from the Student Book that can be used to assess student progress through the section
- a list of general resources that could be used to develop the teaching and learning from that section (Section A).

To enable you to track your coverage of the specifications, and to build in links with the AQA GCSE English and GCSE English Language specifications, some possible routes through the materials are suggested on pages ix–x.

Online resources

The online resources are available on **kerboodle!** which can be accessed via the internet at **www.kerboodle.com/live**, anytime, anywhere.

If your school or college subscribes to **kerboodle!** you and your students will be provided with your own personal login details. Once logged in, access your course and locate the required activity.

Throughout the Student Book and Teacher's Book you will see this icon **k!** whenever there is a relevant interactive activity available in **kerboodle!**. Also, within **kerboodle!** you'll find chapter-by-chapter guidance on how to use each interactive activity, along with additional worksheets to enhance the material from the Student Book.

Please visit **http://kerboodle.helpserve.com** if you would like more information and help on how to use **kerboodle!**.

Finding a route through the materials

The sections and chapters in this resource can be used flexibly with students according to the skills you need to focus on with individual students or groups, or the poems and short stories that you are studying. However, you might find the following notes useful to help you decide which chapters will meet particular teaching and learning targets and which will most appeal to your students.

Links to GCSE English and GCSE English Language

The Nelson Thornes Poetry and Anthology resources can be used as the basis for the study of short stories and poetry for GCSE English Unit 3a Understanding Creative Texts or GCSE English Language Unit 3a Extended reading. In addition, many of the activities provide opportunities to make links with the assessment requirements of English and English Language. These are outlined in the table below.

Section B

Activities (Student Book page no.)	Link to GCSE English	Link to GCSE English Language
7: Characters and Voices, page 52 Stretch yourself: Writing a dialogue between the two young ladies in 'The Ruined Maid' by Thomas Hardy	Unit 2: Speaking and listening – Role playing Unit 3b: Producing creative texts – Prompts and re-creations	Unit 2: Speaking and listening – Role playing Unit 3b: Extended reading – Re-creations
7: Characters and Voices, page 55 Stretch yourself: Writing a short story based on the poem 'Brendon Gallacher' by Jackie Kay	Unit 3b: Producing creative texts – Prompts and re-creations	Unit 3b: Extended reading – Re-creations
8: Place, page 66 Stretch yourself: Rewriting 'London' by William Blake using positive adjectives	Unit 3b: Producing creative texts – Prompts and re-creations	Unit 3b: Extended reading – Re-creations
9: Conflict, page 81 Stretch yourself: Writing a newspaper article on the finding at Mametz Wood	Unit 1B: Producing non-fiction texts	Unit 1B: Producing non-fiction texts
9: Conflict, page 84 Stretch yourself: Writing an account of the battle from the point of view of one of the soldiers involved in 'The Charge of the Light Brigade' by Tennyson	Unit 3b: Producing creative texts – Prompts and re-creations	Unit 3b: Extended reading – Re-creations
9: Conflict, page 86 Stretch yourself: Writing an eye-witness account of the explosion in 'Belfast Confetti' by Ciaran Carson	Unit 3b: Producing creative texts – Prompts and re-creations	Unit 3b: Extended reading – Re-creations
9: Conflict, page 89 Stretch yourself: Writing a poem based on 'Hawk Roosting' by Ted Hughes	Unit 3b: Producing creative texts – Prompts and re-creations	Unit 3b: Extended reading – Re-creations
10: Relationships, page 96 Stretch yourself: Writing a praise song	Unit 3b: Producing creative texts – Prompts and re-creations	Unit 3b: Extended reading – Re-creations
10: Relationships, page 98 Activity 8: Writing a sonnet based on someone or something admired greatly	Unit 3b: Producing creative texts – Prompts and re-creations	Unit 3b: Extended reading – Re-creations

Section C

Activities (Student Book page no.)	Link to GCSE English	Link to GCSE English Language
14: 'The Darkness Out There', page 134 Stretch yourself: Writing a diary entry from the point of view of Kerry and Mrs Rutter	Unit 3b: Producing creative texts – Prompts and re-creations	Unit 3b: Extended reading – Re-creations
15: 'Compass and Torch', page 139 Stretch yourself: Writing a diary entry from the point of view of the boy in the story	Unit 3b: Producing creative texts – Prompts and re-creations	Unit 3b: Extended reading – Re-creations
15: 'Compass and Torch', page 139 Stretch yourself: Role playing a conversation between two of the characters in the story	Unit 2: Speaking and listening – Role playing	Unit 2: Speaking and listening – Role playing
16: 'Anil', page 145 Stretch yourself: Hotseating characters from the story	Unit 2: Speaking and listening – Role playing	Unit 2: Speaking and listening – Role playing
16: 'Anil', page 146 Stretch yourself: Writing a letter from the point of view of the father	Unit 3b: Producing creative texts – Prompts and re-creations	Unit 3b: Extended reading – Re-creations

In addition, many of the activities lend themselves to practice at discussing and listening for Unit 2 Speaking and listening for GCSE English or GCSE English Language, for example, Chapter 1 Getting to grips with poems, Activity 1: Group discussion on responses to 'As Bad as a Mile' by Philip Larkin.

Links to the AQA scheme of work

The resources in each chapter of Section B can be used as starting points to support the scheme of work for Unit 2/Unit 5 published on the AQA website http://web.aqa.org.uk/resourceZone/englishLit.php. In each case, the activities in the Student Book and kerboodle! can be used to introduce and engage students with the poems and can be used alongside suggestions in the scheme of work.

Topic outline	Relevant resources from the Student Book and *kerboodle!*
Overview of the cluster with analysis of one poem	• Introductory Activity: Introducing the topic of place (page 60) • Activities 1–8: analysis of 'Cold Knap Lake' by Gillian Clarke (page 61–62)
Engaging with a second poem from 'Place'	• Activities 1–10: analysis of 'The Wild Swans at Coole' by W B Yeats (page 63–64)
Making a case for including a poem in the Anthology	• Following on from the last piece of work, students could use one of the two poems already studied. • Alternatively, move on to Activities 1–9 based on 'London' by William Blake (page 65–66)
Storyboarding a poem	• Activities 1–12: Analysis of 'Spellbound' by Emily Brontë (page 67–68)
Presenting a poem as drama	• Of the two poems remaining in the Student Book, students could choose to focus on either: • 'Wind' by Ted Hughes, Activities 1–8 (page 68–71) • 'Neighbours' by Gillian Clarke, Activities 1–12 (page 71–73)

Section A: Reading poetry

The Unseen question

Though it might seem initially daunting, the requirement for students to write about an unseen poem in the new specification ought to be seen by both teachers and students as a positive and exciting development.

It will be liberating for teachers because they will be free to design their own programmes of study, thus increasing their 'ownership' of the curriculum. Literary canons are arbitrary, and in even the most carefully designed anthology of poems, the compilers' choice is subjective. Teachers will now be able to follow their personal enthusiasms and tailor their selections of material to students' identified needs and interests. Students usually respond best to texts dealing with issues with which they can identify, and any poem that combines accessibility with challenge will be an appropriate subject for study.

Its value for students is that it will encourage them to become independent learners; they will acquire skills rather than knowledge, and develop a critical reading approach which they can apply to prescribed as well as unseen texts. For a number of years, examiners have complained that students tend to write mechanically on prescribed poems and that in examinations they are often unable to unravel the annotations which they made several months earlier. Moreover, the desire for second-hand 'right answers' and a lack of independent learning skills are criticisms often levelled at students, and not only English students, at A Level and beyond.

It does not take long to read a poem, but to read it with understanding does, because the text must be reread and scrutinised before it yields all its secrets. Being short, poems lend themselves to complete study in single lessons; being concise and sometimes cryptic, they provide powerful stimuli for interactive group work. You can only understand a poem by analysing the writer's use of language in detail, and so the study of poetry fosters close reading skills – skills which will enhance students' achievement in other areas of the curriculum.

Assessment Objectives

There are only two Assessment Objectives for the Unseen paper:

AO1: Respond to texts critically and imaginatively; select and evaluate relevant textual detail to illustrate and support interpretations.

AO2: Explain how language, structure and form contribute to writers' presentation of ideas, themes and settings.

Students will, therefore (in the form of a short critical essay) be invited to demonstrate that they understand *what* a poet is trying to say – to explain the themes, ideas and feelings that the poet is exploring – and comment on the *methods* used by the poet to convey the poem's content effectively, supporting their comments with detailed textual reference. Students will only have to write about one poem, comparison being an Assessment Objective covered only in the Anthology question.

'Respond to texts critically and imaginatively' implies the value of freshness and independence of thought. There is no mention of the word 'device' in the AOs, and students should be discouraged from 'device-spotting'. While a critical vocabulary is ultimately valuable in enabling students to write precisely and concisely, it is possible to interpret figurative language for instance without using technical terms: better to analyse the impact of a 'comparison' than merely identify a metaphor.

The examination questions will be written to reflect the structure of the two AOs (on the lines of 'What is the poet saying about x ... and how do they present ideas and feelings about x effectively?'). For both Higher and Foundation Tiers, their predictable form of words will give students confidence in understanding what they are required to do.

Using this section of the Student Book

The Unseen section has been placed first in the book for the obvious reason that teachers will only wish to prepare students for set poems in the Anthology cluster they have chosen after they have given them extensive practice at exploring poems in a less constrained context. Student's will then come to the set poems more confident and equipped with a critical approach to poetry, even if it is not completely polished. If teachers plan to use the controlled assessment option for poetry, it likewise makes sense for this controlled assessment piece to be attempted only after students have had extensive poetry appreciation practice.

Although it is hoped that the Unseen section meets a range of students' exam preparation needs, it should not be seen as a complete course which needs no further supplementation, nor can it be seen as simply servicing the needs of Anthology poetry study. This is particularly true of Chapter 5, where it is impossible to deal with a variety of verse forms in a short chapter of a textbook. Thus the sonnet form needs to be studied where the sonnet is set. Rather, Section A should be seen as offering a short course 'model' which suggests approaches for teachers to use or modify with poems of their choice. The key to success in the Unseen section of the examination will be wide reading and regular reinforcement of skills.

It is also hoped that the Unseen section has a coherence and logical sequence; it is recommended that students work through the chapters sequentially, particularly since reference is sometimes made to poems used in earlier chapters. There is generally an element of 'stepping' in the sequence of activities within a chapter.

It will become clear on working through the Section that it has a rationale based on several coherent principles:

- Poems chosen are generally 'fresh'.
- Active reading is the focus throughout.
- The importance of pair/group work is continually emphasised.
- Examination skills such as annotation and writing comments supported by quotations are frequently modelled.
- The emphasis on use of technical vocabulary is deliberately restricted.
- Students are encouraged to be confident and adventurous in developing personal and critical responses.

Where oral exercises are indicated, and that is for the majority of activities, they are set as paired activities simply for organisational convenience in the classroom. Experienced teachers will wish to adapt these exercises in more sophisticated ways to cater for larger groups. For ideas on different structures for group work, inexperienced teachers will find the N.A.T.E. booklet *Teaching, Talking and Learning in KS3* (equally valid for KS4) an invaluable source of support.

Active approaches to reading

Within Section A, you will encounter a range of suggested reading approaches, supplemented by further recommendations of texts which suit those approaches in the specific Teacher's Book chapter notes. Approaches which avoid comprehension-type tasks and engage students in active reading activities include:

- cloze procedure – erasing key words and phrases from poems and asking students to predict the missing words; useful for studying diction and imagery
- sequencing – 'jumbling' the sequence of lines or stanzas and challenging students to work out the correct order; useful for examining structure
- question-framing – asking students to devise key questions about poems, exchange with a partner and answer; useful for nurturing a general 'interrogative' approach and focusing on the salient aspects of a poem (see Worksheet 1b: 'Asking the right questions')
- statement evaluation – asking students whether they agree, disagree or don't know whether statements about a poem are true; useful for focusing on writers' intentions (you can include deliberately 'wrong' statements to discourage superficiality in reading)
- 'title prediction' – asking students to work out the title of a poem; useful for encouraging exploration of theme
- 'ending prediction' – offering students poems with the last line or lines removed and asking them to 'complete' the poem; useful for examining theme and structure.

The highlights of teaching poetry appreciation are those moments when students offer valid textual interpretations not previously considered by the teacher, sometimes bringing personal experience and knowledge to bear on the subject in question; students like Robert, the angling enthusiast, who once educated his English teacher about the subtler nuances of Seamus Heaney's 'Trout'.

Successful schools are identified by good teaching. Unfortunately, this sometimes encourages students to think of learning as a passive activity; good English teaching involves the creation of active learning opportunities for students. If such opportunities can be created, students should gain a deep and lasting appreciation of poetry.

Further resources

A teachers' book which helpfully illustrates some of the above and other approaches, though on poems set for the last AQA Anthology, is *Studying AQA Poetry – Comparative Approaches* (English and Media Centre, 2004). Other ways of introducing poems interactively can be found on the AQA website. The analysis of song lyrics might interest students and encourage them to make links with popular culture, and, if you can find appropriate material, you might like to invite students to compare poems with the pictures which inspired them. For instance, W H Auden's 'Musée des Beaux Arts' is based on Breughel's 'The Fall of Icarus', and U A Fanthorpe's 'Not My Best Side' was inspired by Uccello's 'St. George and the Dragon'.

The modern poetry scene is perhaps more vibrant than it has ever been, and advances in printing technology have led to the burgeoning of small presses which offer sources of interesting material. Of these, the most prominent is Bloodaxe Press, whose anthologies *Being Alive*, *Staying Alive* and *The New Poetry* are well worth a browse. Other stimulating teaching anthologies are *Wordlife* (Richard Knott, Nelson), and a Channel 4 Schools Publication *Visible Voices*. It goes without saying that there is a wealth of poetry in old AQA anthologies, new to students if not to teachers, and recommendations for use of selected poems are made in the chapter notes.

Nelson Thornes resources

Chapter	Student Book poems and activities	(k!) resources
1. Getting to grips with poems	**A. Thinking about questions** 'As Bad as a Mile' by Philip Larkin 1–3: First impressions of a poem and starting to think about questions Stretch yourself: the importance of a title **B. Asking your own questions** 'Remembering St. Mary's Churchyard' by Mick Gowar 1–3: Asking questions to establish the poet's intention **C. Backing up your ideas** 'A Woman's Work' by Dorothy Nimmo 1: Using evidence from the poem to back up an opinion Stretch yourself: Using questions in poetry **D. Developing an interpretation** 'The Locker' by John Lancaster 1: Discussing first impressions 2–3: Finding out more about the speaker in a poem Check your learning: Selecting a poem and explaining how it makes you feel and why this is	Interactive activity: What is poetry? Interactive activity: Poem titles and first lines Analysis activity: Analysing meaning in poetry Worksheet 1a: How to read a poem Worksheet 1b: Asking the right questions Worksheet 1c: Activity C PDF versions of the poems included Audio recordings of a selection of the poems included
2. Word choices	**A. Communicating feelings** 1: Rewriting sentences to change the mood and tone	Interactive activity: Changing the tone of a description Interactive activity: Word choices in Owen

Chapter	Student Book poems and activities	k! resources
2. Word choices *continued*	**B. Creating mood** 'Conquerors' by Henry Treece 1: Selecting adjectives that create mood and explaining their effects 2: Annotating a descriptive passage from the poem 3: Linking the speaker to the theme of the poem 4: Suggesting reasons for the title of the poem **C. Thinking about titles** 'Night nurses in the Morning' by Sheenagh Pugh 1–3: Making links between titles and themes **D. Descriptive language** 1: Identifying effective descriptive language 2: Discussing the effects of descriptive words 3: Looking at word choices to write an explanation of the key ideas Stretch yourself: Identifying ways in which poets create sympathy in their readers **E. The sounds of words** 1: Exploring sound techniques **F. Sounds and sound patterns** 1–2: Identifying sound effects and the ways poets use them Check your learning: Looking at how word choices can create a particular atmosphere	Analysis activity: Exploring language in 'Conquerors' and 'Night Nurses in the Morning' Interactive activity: Word choices in Hardy and Keats Interactive activity: Responding to 'Under the Motorway' by U A Fanthorpe Analysis activity: The effect of language Interactive activity: Responding to 'Trout' by Seamus Heaney PDF versions of the poems included Audio recordings of a selection of the poems included
3. Creating pictures with words	**A. Poetic images** 1–2: Analysing and annotating poetic images **B. Snapshots of scenes** 'Calendar' by Owen Sheers 1–2: Identifying images in each stanza and linking the structure of the poem with the images Stretch yourself: Creating your own images **C. Language choices** 'The Face of Hunger' by Oswald Mbuyiseni Mtshali 1–2: Analysing word choices in the poem and their effectiveness 3–4: Discussing the emotive impact of a poem **D. Different types of image** **E. Extending an image** 'The Thickness of Ice' by Liz Loxley 1–2: Analysing the development of an image across a poem 3–4: Using evidence from the poem to support views about it Check your learning: Examining the meaning and effect of an image	Interactive activity: Examining imagery Interactive activity: Responding to imagery in 'Wind' by Ted Hughes Interactive activity: Creating metaphor Interactive activity: Metaphor and meaning Analysis activity: Exploring imagery in 'By St Thomas Water' by Charles Causley Viewpoints activity: 'The Sick Rose' by William Blake Worksheet 3a: Activity E2 PDF versions of the poems included Audio recordings of a selection of the poems included
4. How poems are organised	**A. A typical structure** 'Street Gang' by H Webster 1: Using clues in the opening of a poem to find out more about it 2: Analysing the ending of a poem 3: Thinking about the impact of pace **B. Using contrast** 'The Boys and Girls Are Going out to Play' by Dorothy Nimmo 1–3: Analysing the structure of a poem and the poet's intentions behind it Stretch yourself: Reflecting on gender stereotypes within the poem	Interactive activity: Effects of structure in 'O what is that sound' by W H Auden Interactive activity: Responding to structure in 'An Irish Airman foresees his Death' by W B Yeats Analysis activity: Exploring structure in 'The Convergence of the Twain' by Thomas Hardy Analysis activity: Exploring structure in 'Book Ends' by Tony Harrison

Chapter	Student Book poems and activities	🇰! resources
4. How poems are organised *continued*	**C. Out of order** 'Disabled' by Wilfred Owen 1–2: Reordering stanzas of a poem to assess impact of structure on meaning 3–5: Exploring the poet's use of past and present to structure the poem 6: Analysing the ending of the poem and the impact this has on the reader Check your learning: Looking at structure in 'Night and Morning' by R S Thomas	Viewpoints activity: 'Halley's Comet' by Stanley Kunitz PDF versions of the poems included Audio recordings of a selection of the poems included
5. The best words in the best order	**A. Poems that rhyme** 'Another Christmas Poem' by Wendy Cope 'Wires' by Philip Larkin 1–4: Exploring the rhyme-scheme of a poem, its impact and how this links to the poet's theme Stretch yourself: Analysing the placement of phrases in the poem and the impact these have **B. Word placement** 'Drummer Hodge' by Thomas Hardy 1–2: Identifying rhyming patterns and how the poet uses these to structure the poem 3–5: Commenting on the poet's choice of, and placement of, words and the impact that these have **C. Free verse** 'The Pond' by Owen Sheers 1–3: Analysing how the poet emphasises words and phrases with the use of enjambement and the effects of these **D. Prose into verse** 'Living Space' by Imtiaz Dharker 1–2: Structure a prose version of the poem into free verse 3: Commenting on the impact of the poet's choice to write free verse Check your learning: Studying a haiku to see the effects of word placement	Interactive activity: The best words for the best sounds Interactive activity: Rhyme and rhythm in 'The Eagle' by Alfred, Lord Tennyson Interactive activity: Rhyme and rhythm in 'Meeting at Night' by Robert Browning Analysis activity: Exploring word placement in 'The Song of Hiawatha' by Henry Wadsworth Longfellow Interactive activity: Line placement in 'Anthem for Doomed Youth' by Wilfred Owen Viewpoints activity: 'Tall Nettles' by Edward Thomas Analysis activity: Exploring rhyme and repetition in 'Do not go gentle into that good night' by Dylan Thomas PDF versions of the poems included Audio recordings of a selection of the poems included
6. Making your skills count in the exam: the Unseen question	**Sample question** 1–2: Identifying key words and phrases in a poem to answer the exam style questions 3: Comparing with the suggested response 4: Writing a response to an exam-style question 5: Analysing a sample student response with examiner comments	Analysis activity: Analysing poems about parents and children Analysis activity: Analysing sonnets Analysis activity: Analysing animal poems Analysis activity: Analysing voice in poems Planning activity: 'Nettles' Planning activity: 'Bayonet Charge' On your marks activity: 'Granny Scarecrow' PDF versions of the poems included (plus annotated version) Audio recordings of a selection of the poems included

1 Getting to grips with poems

 Interactive activity: What is poetry?

AO focus

AO1: Respond to texts critically and imaginatively; select and evaluate relevant textual detail to illustrate and support interpretation.

AO2: Explain how language, structure and form contribute to writers' presentation of ideas, themes and settings.

In this chapter your students will:

- learn to think about the meaning of poems
- learn to ask questions that help them to interpret poems
- learn to back up their interpretation with evidence from the poem.

Key terms

Key terms the students are introduced to in this chapter:

- Interpret
- Intention
- Justify

Poems included in this chapter

'As Bad as a Mile' by Philip Larkin

In the following chapters, an attempt has been made to 'step' poems in levels of difficulty. The rationale for beginning with this challenging 'philosophical' poem is that:

- it is short, and can quickly be reread several times
- carefully targeted questions are provided to support students
- students will be able to see the relevance of the sporting comparison (Activity 2)
- the conciseness of the poem demonstrates clearly how poetry can 'say a lot in a little'.

Philip Larkin was born in 1922 and died in 1985. He was offered the post of Poet Laureate in 1984, but he did not accept the position because of the media attention that it would bring.

'Remembering St Mary's Churchyard' by Mick Gowar

Both the language and content of this poem are accessible. It makes demands on students' emotional maturity rather than intellectual prowess, and is suitable for mixed ability groups.

'A Woman's Work' by Dorothy Nimmo

Again, students of all abilities should be comfortable with the level of challenge presented by this poem. It might be helpful to preface study of the poem with a pre-reading activity on gender stereotypes. Perhaps students could list and compare their ideas on domestic 'chores' usually carried out by male partner/female partner/both.

Dorothy Nimmo's poems and short stories have been published in a variety of anthologies and magazines. She died in 2001.

'The Locker' by John Lancaster

As explained in the notes that follow, the reason this poem works so well is that it offers challenge to able students without in any way excluding less able students.

Additional resources

Worksheets:

- Ia: How to read a poem
- Ib: Asking the right questions
- Ic: Activity C

PDF versions of all poems featured in this chapter are available for annotation purposes.

Audio recordings of some of the poems used in this chapter are also available in the online resource.

Getting started

In this chapter students practise interpreting the 'meaning', or possible meanings of poems. They are encouraged to be self-confident, adventurous, and to develop the 'knack' of asking focused questions. Most of the poems chosen are ambiguous and intended to promote exploratory talk. The use of technical vocabulary is deliberately avoided at this stage.

Students are introduced to the idea that there is no 'fixed' meaning to a poem at the beginning of this chapter; people respond in different ways to poetry. They are reassured that there is no 'wrong' interpretation and that as long as they can back up their arguments with evidence from the text, their interpretation will be valid. A personal response to the text is something the examiner will be looking for and is explicitly covered in Section B of the Student Book; here, students are encouraged to engage with the text and formulate a substantiated response. Students may initially feel daunted about analysing poetry and so this chapter opens with guidance on how to build their confidence through sustained practice.

The first section of this chapter introduces students to the importance of asking pertinent questions when interpreting poetry. Through close analysis students will learn to move beyond first impressions and develop more rounded interpretations.

Working through the chapter

A. Thinking about questions

Activities A1–A3 These activities are intended as an opening set of short tasks in which students are guided through the process of finding textual clues in 'As Bad as a Mile' by Philip Larkin to help them to make sense of what initially might seem a rather puzzling poem. The idea is that if you identify clues and can think of the 'right' questions, you can discern the poet's intentions.

With help, students should eventually conclude that the poem explores the idea that when people fail to achieve their aims, they often explain failure away as bad luck. The more they fail, even if narrowly, the more they have to face the truth. They often mistakenly comfort themselves by thinking that if they could go back in time and have another chance, they would be successful.

Stretch yourself

Interactive activity: Poem titles and first lines
This activity is intended to encourage students to think about specific words in a poem's title in relation to its theme. The title offers no helpful clues as to what the poem is about, and is, in fact, rather puzzling. However, because the reader is so familiar with the original cliché, the obvious change would arrest the reader's attention, and be thought-provoking. 'A miss is as good as a mile' suggests that failure is failure, however near the miss might be. Presumably the poet's choice of 'bad' rather than 'good' enhances the poem's pessimistic tone; there is nothing good about missing.

Other features of the poem to consider might be:

- the effects of repetition in the poem – how 'less and less' and 'more and more' emphasise the sense of personal failure

- the emphatic position at the beginning of the stanza of 'Of failure', which follows the repetition noted above

- why an apple might have been chosen (the Garden of Eden and the concept of Original Sin).

B. Asking your own questions

Students are reminded to think about the points raised in the Section A Introduction about how to approach a poem before reading the next poem in this chapter: 'Remembering St. Mary's Churchyard' by Mick Gowar. These guidance points are summarised on Worksheet 1a: How to read a poem.

Activity B1 This activity is intended to encourage students to focus on formulating pertinent questions to interpret meaning successfully. If the questions provided for the Larkin poem succeeded in helping the reader to 'tease out' meaning, it follows that by developing questioning skills students can become more effective independent readers. It also invites students to begin to think about *themes*.

This activity offers good opportunities for Speaking and listening assessment and could be done in other group structures, e.g. a pair collaborating to create questions and joining up with another pair to discuss answers.

Question-framing activities can be very effective in building self-confidence. At the end, you can often point out how much students have 'taught' themselves with limited teacher intervention.

This task is likely to be done more effectively if you discuss question-framing beforehand, and emphasise that questions should be challenging and lead to developed answers ('why?' not 'what?' questions). You may wish to put examples of effectively probing and less challenging questions on the board to demonstrate the point, perhaps based on the Larkin poem (or use Worksheet 1b: 'Asking the right questions').

Activity B2 This activity is intended to give students an opportunity to formalise a general interpretation of a poem briefly – a prelude to writing more developed responses as they gain experience.

Plenary discussion, or additional questions you may feel the need to pose, might focus on the reasons for the boys' detachment from the girl's situation/behaviour, for instance their lack of experience/maturity, and their absorption in their world of play.

Activity B3 This activity is intended to build on students' response to Activity B2 by asking them to focus specifically on the speaker's and his friend's attitude to the girl. Students should be encouraged to find textual detail from the poem to support points about how the poet demonstrates their immaturity. Some students may not feel that the speaker and his friends have acted in an immature way so this could generate some interesting discussion.

Other interesting features to discuss include:

- the significance of the title. Might the poem be autobiographical? Is the implication that the speaker as an adult can see his insensitivity as a child?

- the children's sense of time as described in the early parts of the poem compared with the implications of time for the girl: there is no time pressure on them, they are absolutely carefree; whereas now that the girl is pregnant, time moves her inexorably towards a significant point in her life. The contrasting child/adult views of time are highlighted by 'in what adults thought/a ten minute walk at most'

- the leisurely style in the first part of the poem (long, unpunctuated lines, detailed description) compared with the more terse, urgent style in the second part, which perhaps reflects the time issue highlighted above

- the patterned repetition, especially of questions, which emphasises the boys' lack of comprehension, almost incredulity

- the specific effects of the free verse form in creating emphases

- the pivotal nature of 'But never did', which moves the poem in another direction, and the finality of the last line 'forgot her'

- what and why the girl might have been intending to use the ('untouched') sketch-pad for – to draw, write to the father, her parents, a friend, etc.

C. Backing up your ideas

Activity C1 This activity is intended to help students to understand that, while poems do not have 'fixed meanings', and are open to varied interpretations, some interpretations make more sense than others, and convincing interpretations are ones that are justified, using textual detail. In addition, it helps them to learn that not everything a poet says can be taken at face value, which introduces the notion of *irony*.

This type of statement evaluation activity works well with poems which contain irony, as students have to respond to tone and 'look beneath the surface'.

Most students would agree with the suggested response to the first statement. The eighth statement is obviously not true, but designed to make students consider literal/figurative meaning; the seashore is a metaphor for freedom – a new journey or adventure.

The remainder of the statements invite more open-ended responses. Stanza 3 suggests that the husband left home – should she have been strong and left him first in view of his behaviour? There are issues to discuss here about the possible financial implications of her position; would she be likely to be financially independent? Although the last stanza emphasises freedom, the husband's departure has left 'an empty space', so there are losses and gains as a result of his departure.

This activity is replicated on Worksheet 1c in the online resources.

Stretch yourself This activity is intended to help students to perceive that meaning is often conveyed *implicitly* – the changes in how the woman speaks reveal changes in her attitudes and feelings.

Other noteworthy features of the poem are:

- the use of the short, emphatic refrain, significantly modified in the last stanza, where frustration and despondency change to assertiveness

- the predominance of questions in the first two stanzas compared with the assertive use of verbs in the final stanza ('I find', 'I lock'), which mark the speaker's 'self-discovery'

Students interested by the 'gender' issues in the poem might like to read 'High Flier', by the same poet, Dorothy Nimmo.

D. Developing an interpretation

Analysis activity: Analysing meaning in poetry

Activity D1 This activity asks students to discuss their first impressions of the poem.

Note how pivotal the isolated short third stanza is:

'There could be nothing to expect
When the gate-man gave her the locker key.'

'Mother must never know of course' generates an interesting discussion about the speaker's identity. If the speaker is the daughter, she obviously wants to protect her mother; if the speaker is the wife, she might not want to worry her mother, 'wash her dirty linen in public', and destroy her mother's illusions about her son-in-law, etc.

The last stanza is important: the woman is like a locker, her heart containing a secret, possibly to be locked away for ever.

The poem contains relatively little imagery, but 'excursion' (an enjoyable day out before returning to routine – not even a sustained holiday), 'evaporate' (forgetting and forgiving isn't easy; the problem won't simply disappear) and the locker metaphor are more subtle than they at first seem.

Activity D2 This activity is intended to give students the opportunity to put into practice what they have learned about asking questions and supporting interpretations in a more sustained and open-ended way.

It works because of the poem's central ambiguity: a case can be made for the speaker being either wife or daughter, and students will find arguments rooted in the text and in their interpretations of the psychology of the speaker. You might not require students to do any writing.

An alternative approach to this activity is to prepare two simple worksheets with the task 'Trace the development of the wife's/daughter's feelings in the poem'. Distribute the two versions between pairs (and then groups of four) and wait for students to discover the discrepancy and argue the different cases.

Activity D3 This activity is intended to focus students' attention on important textual details which need to be interpreted if they are to understand the subtle development of the woman's thoughts and feelings.

This activity is intended to enable students to make a first attempt at formalising an extended response to a poem – orally, at this stage – without having it formally assessed. Having the accounts read gives the teacher opportunities to reinforce the importance of the use of textual detail to support ideas by identifying and praising good practice, and asking for further clarification of ideas asserted but not justified.

The poem is accessible but subtle, and the quality of exploratory talk it stimulates is usually such that the teacher can become redundant! It is also a good confidence booster, because at the end of the activity you can point out to the students how well they have understood the poem through group interaction, with minimal teacher direction.

Check your learning This activity is intended to provide students with some choice in offering a more personal (but informed) response, whilst briefly reinforcing what they have learned about how they might interpret a poem's 'meaning'.

Further reading

Other poems useful for studying meaning include:

- Robert Frost's 'Fire and Ice', a compact nine-line poem which uses metaphor/symbolism to explore the destructive potential of passion and hatred. It is more suitable for Higher Tier students.
- Robert Frost's 'The Road Not Taken', which uses the metaphor of the road to explore people's choices of path in life. It is suitable for Foundation Tier students.

Outcomes

In this chapter students have:

- learned that 'meaning' in poems is not something fixed
- practised asking pertinent questions to tease out meaning
- learned that valid interpretations need to be supported.

AO focus

AO1: Respond to texts critically and imaginatively; select and evaluate relevant textual detail to illustrate and support interpretation.

AO2: Explain how language, structure and form contribute to writers' presentation of ideas, themes and settings.

In this chapter your students will:

- learn how words can be used to suggest feelings
- learn how patterns of words can create mood and atmosphere.

Key terms

Key terms the students are introduced to in this chapter:

- Tone
- Adjective
- Annotate
- Irony
- Stanza
- Onomatopoeia
- Consonant
- Alliteration
- Assonance

Poems included in this chapter

'Conquerors' by Henry Treece

This poem makes a good starting point for studying a poet's vocabulary choices, as, though it does explore ideas, it is essentially descriptive and very detailed. The language is accessible, and students of all abilities should find the poem approachable. The subtlety that would stretch the more able students lies in the irony of the situation, discussed in the notes below.

Henry Treece was born in 1911 and served as an intelligence officer in the Royal Air Force in the Second War War. He died in 1966.

'Night Nurses in the Morning' by Sheenagh Pugh

The content of this poem ought to interest students of all abilities, but it is probably best prepared orally in mixed ability groups, as a less

able pair might find it difficult. There is more sophisticated vocabulary to be explained here, and the poem moves from description to more complex reflection. Although Activity D3 will focus students' thinking, they will need teacher support in order to grasp fully the meaning of the concluding two lines.

Sheenagh Pugh was born in 1950. She taught creative writing until her retirement in 2008.

'The Classroom' by John Mole

This poem is used in the Check your learning activity at the end of the chapter and contains some excellent examples of onomatopoeic language.

Additional resources

PDF versions of all poems featured in this chapter are available for annotation purposes.

Audio recordings of some of the poems used in this chapter are also available in the online resources.

Getting started

In this chapter students study diction – poets' choice of words, often as part of a pattern – and its role in creating particular effects and suggesting mood and atmosphere, sometimes by being emotive.

A. Communicating feelings

This chapter opens with an exploration of how a person's tone and choice of language can indicate how they are feeling, as well as communicate information.

> **Activity A1**
>
> Interactive activity: Changing the tone of a description

This activity is intended to encourage students to start thinking about the effects of certain word choices and how these choices can alter meaning.

Obviously any relevant 'positive' words in part (a) or 'negative' words in part (b) will be acceptable in responses. Ask students to read examples out and praise instances of precise, vivid vocabulary. Alternatively, ask students to share in pairs and recommend good examples written by their partners.

Working through the chapter

B. Creating mood

Activity B1

Interactive activity: Word choices in Owen

This activity is intended to illustrate, using the poem 'Conquerors', how the cumulative effects of a poet's language choices – especially adjectives – can create a particular mood.

The language of the poem is accessible. Students should have little difficulty in identifying the variety of 'negative' adjectives which indicate desolation and privation. The activity could be given a brisk time target.

Examples of adjectives that students could suggest include: 'broken', 'dead', 'rusting', 'tattered', 'weed-grown', 'gaunt', 'dark', 'grey' and 'shattered'.

You are now in a position to discuss with students how it is the accumulation of detail, creating a 'pattern', which creates the pervasive mood.

Activity B2

This activity is intended to focus students' attention on the poet's use of descriptive details by annotating a section of 'Conquerors' and explaining the effects of the poet's use of language.

A suitable comment might be: "The poet is trying to make us feel sorry for the dog, which has little flesh on its bones; its face is 'gaunt' and its legs are 'as thin as sticks'. You can imagine its legs like pieces of bamboo, with the thin legs emphasising the knee joints. 'Shambled' suggests that the dog is aimless; it is clearly going off 'to die'. (Note that 'at least in peace' implies that some of the people conquered might have a less calm end to their lives.)"

Throughout the Student Book, students are asked to study annotated passages of poem text and to annotate sections themselves, so this is a straightforward poem where students can start to build on this skill.

Activity B3

This activity again asks students to look closely at a particular passage from 'Conquerors' and encourages them to think about the speaker's implicit feelings.

A suitable comment might be: "Although the 'enemy', the soldiers have not been so desensitised by war that they have lost sympathy for a vulnerable, innocent child. During the war, they probably had to kill people they saw as enemies to survive – but it is likely the war was not of their own making."

Activity B4

This activity introduces students to the significance of poem titles and asks them to consider whether everything a poet says can be taken at face value. It also prepares students to think about the implications of the title of the next poem in this chapter.

The title is ironic, of course; the soldiers are not made happy by victory. The last few lines of the poem, with the reference to the 'grey child' subtly show the soldiers' humanity now that they have been removed from a situation where they have to kill or be killed. The first statement is clearly wrong – the mood created is hardly celebratory – but the other two statements can clearly be justified.

This might be a good point at which to introduce students to the notion of the *persona* – a speaker in a poem created by a poet. A persona is like a character created by a dramatist. What the persona says does not necessarily represent what the actual poet thinks and feels. In some cases a poet will deliberately create a persona whose attitudes and behaviour the poet invites the reader to criticise.

C. Thinking about titles

Activity C1

This activity encourages students to think about the irony of poem titles and the difference between the first impression generated by the title and the actual content of a poem. Irony can be quite a difficult concept to grasp for students and so it may be worth spending some time on this to make sure students are clear what it means.

Activity C2

This activity is intended to serve as a pre-reading activity before students study 'Night Nurses in the Morning'. It prepares them to respond empathetically to the description of the nurses' situation in the poem.

Again, in taking oral feedback, you have opportunities to praise effective vocabulary/subtle ideas. It would be possible to develop the 'first draft' from this pre-reading activity into a more sustained piece of 'finished' creative writing, perhaps by broadening the scope of the task, but it is essentially intended to focus students' thinking on the particular topic.

D. Descriptive language

Analysis activity: Exploring language in 'Conquerors' and 'Night Nurses in the Morning'

Another example of effective annotation is presented to students here – highlighting the importance and value of applying focus to a particular technique used by the poet in order to increase understanding. A model of how students can then expand their annotation comments into a paragraph is given.

Activity D1

🔲 Interactive activity: Word choices in Hardy and Keats

🔲 Interactive activity: Responding to 'Under the Motorway' by U A Fanthorpe

This activity focuses on descriptive language in 'Night Nurses in the Morning' and asks students to make a note of which descriptive details they find most effective and why. This encourages personal response and reinforces the need to use evidence from poems to support interpretation.

Explanations might go something like:

Example 1: "The nurses' ankles are swollen because they are on their feet all day, often lifting heavy burdens (e.g. patients). Their shoes look clumsy and functional. They'd like to have their feet soothed and pampered on a health-farm."

Example 2: "Everything in a hospital seems to be pale in colour – perhaps deliberately to soothe the patients – but the nurses' uniform makes them look rather lifeless, drab and lacking identity as individuals."

Example 3: "Colliers stand out because of the coal grime on their faces. Snooker players dress flamboyantly. The nurses' extreme paleness makes them look tired and washed out. They are vampires because they take blood samples, but they do so to make patients better, not prey on them. (There's an interesting implied contrast between the colliers, who do a hard physical job, and the snooker-players, who do not.)"

Activity D2

This activity focuses students' attention on contrasted descriptive details in 'Night Nurses in the Morning' in order to draw their attention to an ambivalence in the speaker's attitudes and feelings towards the nurses.

Example 1 is rather dismissive – somewhere where you put old people to get them 'out of your hair'.

Example 2 shows sympathy for their helplessness.

Example 3 recognises that we too easily 'sweep problems under the carpet' rather than accept social responsibility for people – whose problems we will all eventually face ourselves.

Activity D3

This activity is intended to support students in understanding the 'difficult' conclusion of the poem by providing key questions to focus their thinking.

This is a complex ending to explain. The nurses are so tired that they are not very alert to the world around them, unlike 'normal' people awakening to a new day. We cannot see into their 'souls'. The silver at the back of their eyes is like a barrier to

our understanding of the difficult experiences they face at work. The back of a mirror is made of silver. When we look at their eyes, it is as if we are looking at a mirror; we are forced to look at *ourselves* and our responsibilities more clearly when we think about what they do. We empathise with them and appreciate their value (the other connotation of 'silver').

Students are briefly introduced here to the structure of this poem and its organisational features are listed. They will learn more about the structure of poems in Chapter 4.

Stretch yourself This activity could be attempted by candidates of all abilities, but offers more able students the opportunity to write a reasonably developed justified response without having been given very specific guidance. Students of different abilities might be given different definitions of what 'short' should represent to them.

E. The sounds of words

Although it is logical to consider the sound qualities of words in a chapter on diction, this aspect of poetry is quite difficult for students to grasp at this stage of the course (assuming that chapters are being studied chronologically, which is the author's intention). It is an area in which students are likely to become confident only after undertaking wide reading and having 'lessons' reinforced by their teacher.

In order to provide a range of examples, and to help students focus on sound qualities without having to unravel other aspects of meaning, this part of the book is different in that it uses short 'decontextualised' extracts rather than complete poems.

Here are some very simple tips that will help students think about the sound qualities of words:

- consonant sounds such as 'g', 'k' and (hard) 'c' are usually quite harsh-sounding

- consonant sounds as 'f', 's' and 'p' are usually quite soft-sounding

- words with one syllable and a short vowel sound, like 'hit', often sound abrupt

- words with long vowel sounds, such as 'strained', often create a slow pace in a poem.

A difficulty is that, while there are some general principles which can helpfully be applied, generalisations about the effects of use of letters and combinations of letters do not hold good in all contexts (see the comment at the end of 'Thistles' for example). Consonants may be hard or soft, and their effects need to be evaluated within specific contexts.

Students should be encouraged to read the poem extracts presented here aloud, as this will help them to hear the sounds clearly and understand the effects of the language chosen.

Activity E4 This activity is designed to reinforce students' understanding of the techniques introduced at the opening of the chapter.

Onomatopoeia: the air passing through the water and creating bubbles makes a 'gurgly' sound like someone gargling, but less harshly ('delicately').

Alliteration: the repetition of the 'd' sounds gives the line a heaviness which reflects the dullness and drabness of the day.

Assonance: the repetition of the sound in 'slice' and 'ice' sounds incisive and cold. The snowman is icily cold, and the teenager sees himself as being emotionally cold/'tough'.

F. Sounds and sound patterns

Activity F1 This active is intended to give students further opportunities to respond to sound qualities in poetry. Some examples are more challenging than others, but even less able students should be able to write about one of the last two examples. The easier ones have been left to the end so that students at least attempt the earlier ones. It is not important that students identify techniques by name.

a   The repeated use of 'sh' sounds suggests the sighing sound of the leaves blowing in the wind; the repetition in the very final line has a rhythmical effect which creates a pleasing conclusion to the poem.

b   The 't' and 'sp' sounds give the lines a 'hissing/spitting' quality which reinforces the subject-matter, and the 'hits'/'spits' assonance/internal rhyme gives the key word 'spits' an effective emphasis.

c   The alliterative use of the letter 's' gives the quotation a pace which contrasts the sudden action with the soldiers' endless waiting. The use of other crisp consonants like 't', 'k' and hard 'c' creates emphases which suggest sharp repeated sounds, like those made by bullets.

d   In addition to suggesting a slippery texture, 'slobber' sounds like a jelly-like substance being poured.

e   The onomatopoeic sounds of 'slap' and 'plop' reflect the sounds of the frogs jumping in and out of the water.

Activity F2 This activity asks students to formalise their response to the short extracts by writing an explanation of how the poet uses sounds in one example. Ensure that students are focusing on the effects that the sounds have.

Check your learning

Analysis activity: The effect of language

Interactive activity: Responding to 'Trout' by Seamus Heaney

This activity is intended to reinforce the objectives of this chapter and check students' learning by providing a short question that encompasses multiple elements of the chapter's focus.

The poet is trying to suggest that the classroom is chaotic and there is not a lot of work going on. The words 'deafen', 'clatter', 'crackle', 'glop' and 'gurgle' suggest how noisy it is (some of these words are onomatopoeic) and you can visualise the children's swollen bellies and the array of their colourful gobstoppers, which are like a galaxy.

Further reading

Other poems useful for studying diction include:

- R S Thomas' 'Evans', which uses pathetic fallacy in describing a bleak, lonely setting which is the background for the death of a lonely Welsh hill farmer. It is accessible for Foundation Tier candidates.

- Chinua Achebe's 'Vultures', which again uses pathetic fallacy in creating a bleak setting which harmonises with the sinister behaviour of the scavengers. A good preparatory reading activity is to ask students to highlight separately positive and negative descriptions of both the setting and the vultures in the first half of the poem. This helps the reader to understand the ambiguity explored in the later description of human behaviour. It is a challenging poem more suitable for Higher Tier students because of the complex philosophy explored in the last stanza.

- Gillian Clarke's 'Catrin', which uses contrasted language related to love and conflict to explore a parent/child relationship (which can again be identified by highlighting). The poem uses quite 'abstract' imagery, and is therefore more suited to Higher Tier students. It is useful for supporting study of the 'Relationships' cluster in the Anthology.

- (for sound qualities) poems by Seamus Heaney, Wilfred Owen and Robert Frost.

Outcomes

In this chapter students have learned that:

- words can convey feelings

- patterns of words can create mood and atmosphere

- poets choose words for sound effects.

AO focus

AO1: Respond to texts critically and imaginatively; select and evaluate relevant textual detail to illustrate and support interpretation.

AO2: Explain how language, structure and form contribute to writers' presentation of ideas, themes and settings.

In this chapter your students will:

- learn how poets use images to create descriptions
- learn how images can make them think and feel as well as see
- learn how images can be extended to develop ideas.

Key terms

Key terms the students are introduced to in this chapter:

- Image
- Visualise
- Emotive
- Simile
- Metaphor
- Pun

Poems included in this chapter

'Calendar' by Owen Sheers

The purpose of this poem (i.e. to provide the reader with a series of visual images), and its simple structure, provide a natural sequel to the aims of the previous introductory activities. Its limited focus makes it accessible to all students, and because each stanza can be seen to be doing something similar, the activity's aims are effectively reinforced. More able students will be challenged by thinking about the inter-connection of images in the final stanza.

Owen Sheers was born in 1974. He has been a Poet in Residence for The Poetry Archive. (www. poetryarchive.org carries readings by poets of their own work and contains much useful information and teaching material.) Sheers also presented the 2009 BBC television series 'A Poet's Guide to Britain.'

'The Face of Hunger' by Oswald Mbuyiseni Mtshali

Again, this is an accessible but challenging poem, rich in imagery, whose subject-matter should appeal to students. It extends the work done on visual imagery by demonstrating to students that images can inspire feelings as well as create pictures.

Oswald Mbuyiseni Mtshali is a South African poet born in 1940. He has written poetry in both English and Zulu.

'The Thickness of Ice' by Liz Loxley

Students respond enthusiastically to the subject-matter of this poem, which extends their learning by introducing the poetic technique of structural metaphor. Here they have to think through a *sequence* of ideas developed by aspects of the central image.

Liz Loxley was born in 1961 and was educated in Bristol. She has performed her poetry and has been involved in running poetry workshops for local poetry festivals.

Additional resources

Worksheets:

- 3a: Activity E2

PDF versions of all poems featured in this chapter are available for annotation purposes.

Audio recordings of some of the poems used in this chapter are also available in the online resources.

Getting started

In this chapter students learn to interpret images, including extended metaphors. They first focus on visual images, then consider the emotive power of images, and finally study an extended metaphor to understand how images also make the reader think.

Images are at the very heart of poetry; they are the key tools of a poet's 'trade'. In order to interpret poems, the reader is constantly being challenged to think about what two things compared, explicitly or implicitly, might have in common.

A. Poetic images

🔤 Interactive activity: Examining imagery

Students are introduced to this concept by comparing the poet's way of using words to create imagery with an artist painting a picture with brush and paint. Poets prompt a reader's imagination and appeal to the senses to stimulate the visualisation of poetic images.

Activities A1 and A2 These activities are intended to introduce students to the effects of visual images in poetry by asking them to look at two sections of poetry dealing with a similar theme.

A relevant interpretation of 'Dawn Shoot' would be: 'This image suggests to me that the railway line really stood out. It was dead straight and heading right into the centre of the bridge, like an arrow homing in on its target. The dark hole of the tunnel looked to be staring out at you like an eye.'

The explanation of 'Journey from Hull' might go something like: 'As night falls, the train surges forward powerfully, weaving its way along like a muscular snake.'

As with some other parts of this chapter, an illustration is provided to initiate students' thinking and to engage their attention. However, it must be stressed that students should allow their imagination to 'roam free' and not be inhibited by prescriptive visual aids and so an excessive use of illustrations or photos is avoided in this chapter.

Working through the chapter

B. Snapshots of scenes

🔤 Interactive activity: Responding to imagery in 'Wind' by Ted Hughes

Activity B1 This activity is intended, informally, to draw students' attention to the poem's structure in order to help them more easily grasp its purpose.

There are twelve months in the year; the poet divides his poem into four equal sections of three lines to represent the four seasons, which are seen as being of similar length.

Activity B2 This activity is intended to give students further practice in formalising their interpretations of images.

Examples of possible explanations:

Summer: When a bee pollinates a flower, it moves delicately and tentatively over the plant's surface. As the foxgloves' openings look like lips, the poet sees the bee's movements as being like those of an inexperienced lover 'feeling his way'.

Autumn: The poet suggests that the fragile spider web resembles the delicate interconnected lines of a fingerprint (a fingerprint is light). The lightness and grace of the spider's movements are suggested by the word 'danced', and 'in the space' may imply wonder at the spider's ability to remain 'airborne'.

Winter: The bare branches of the tree, stripped of leaves, stand out starkly against the sky; all connected but moving in different directions like veins in the human body. Likewise the clumps of nests are prominent now that the trees are without their leaves. The rooks come and go, their blackness suggesting signs of disease. Blood clots can lead to death, and so 'clots' and 'infection' are rather sinister. The image is colourless and the blackness seems to symbolise death, though infections can pass in time, and Spring will return.

Stretch yourself This activity is intended to give students the opportunity to put into practice what they have learned about imagery by creating a 'snapshot' of one of the seasons.

This is a short creative activity; students could try out more than one image if time permits, even one for each season. They could focus on the unseasonable nature of weather in some examples. After examples have been shared by the class, they could be collated for display.

Each stanza of 'Calendar' is a haiku. You could study the specific form and ask students to imitate it in creating their images – the discipline might sharpen their thinking.

C. Language choices

This part of the chapter looks at the use of emotive language. An example is given here of an emotive photographic image – a starving child in a developing country – and students are asked to think about how this photo is intended to make them feel. Students usually respond strongly to such photos and so this is an effective task to lead into looking at 'The Face of Hunger', which creates a poetic image of a similar situation. You could extend this by showing your students similarly emotive photographs and asking them to explain the effect that they have and why they think this is, before moving on to look at emotive language in poetry.

Activity C1 This activity is intended to focus students' attention on why the poet uses particular images in specific contexts, at this stage using clues about visual effects. Answers may include:

1 'sky-high' – explained as an example in Activity C2.

2 'a glove on a doctor's hand' – conveys the idea that the skin is stretched so tautly that it is almost transparent, only just concealing the fleshless bones.

3 'a chameleon's' – explained at the opening of 'Different types of image'.

4 'confetti' – a visual image suggesting that the flies are in swarms as if thrown in a bunch (perhaps ironic in that weddings are joyful occasions); 'snatching' is emphatically positioned to suggest desperation.

5 'a den of lions' – suggests violent hunger pangs, which are audible (and the relentlessness of the pain is forcefully conveyed by the final emphatic 'day and night').

A copy of the complete version of the poem can be found at the back of the Student Book and also in the online resources.

Cloze procedures can be very effective in helping students to focus on imagery and diction, provided they don't merely aim to get the answers right without being able to justify poets' language choices. An alternative is not to provide answers, but to ask students to think of their own words to complete a cloze exercise, and then discuss the poet's actual choice of words.

Poems which use vigorous language, such as Seamus Heaney's 'Storm on the Island' and Ted Hughes's 'The Jaguar' and 'Wind' (in the Place cluster of the Anthology) work well as cloze exercises.

Activity C2 This activity is intended to encourage students to think beyond the visual effects of images and understand that images can be emotive, by making a personal response to a selected detail.

Students will probably select from the highlighted images explained above.

Activity C3 This activity links the poem back to the photograph that the students looked at. They are asked to discuss the emotional impact that both the poem and the photo has had on them. This will further increase their confidence when discussing their personal responses.

David Craig's poem 'Save the Children', on a similar theme, is well worth studying alongside this poem.

D. Different types of image

 Interactive activity: Creating metaphor

 Interactive activity: Metaphor and meaning

 Analysis activity: Exploring imagery in 'By St. Thomas Water' by Charles Causley

The difference between simile and metaphor is something which often tests students' minds, and so a full explanation/illustration is included here. However, students are often better at 'spotting' the techniques than explaining their effects, which should be the focus of their learning, and so it is the last paragraph of this explanatory section that needs emphasising.

Studying the effects of different kinds of image in context is a good way of teaching the difference further. 'Calendar', for example, is a good example of how the use of metaphor leads to directness and conciseness, as is the 'Movements' poem referred to in the suggestions for further study.

E. Extending an image

 Viewpoints activity: 'The Sick Rose' by William Blake

This section of the chapter explores how poets can develop their images and apply an extended metaphor to their poems.

Activity E1 This activity is intended to focus on the chronological sequence of the poem, which is important to its meaning.

The time references 'At first', 'Later' and 'Last of all', each repeated to open two stanzas in sequence, make it clear that the poet is describing distinct phases of a developing relationship.

Activity E2 This activity is intended to help students to understand that, as well as creating an incidental 'word-picture', a poet often focuses on separate aspects of an image and uses them to develop more complex thoughts about a situation. The table could be completed as follows:

Stanza	On the surface ...	Deep down ...
3	When we've got to know each other, we'll be more self-confident, less insecure, and take the 'goal' of our relationship for granted.	We'll have got used to each other. We'll have no need to show off any more and just be content with each other's company.
4	We'll become complacent and not notice that we're not as warm towards each other or that there are weaknesses in our relationship.	And so when our relationship collapses, it'll be sudden and unexpected. We'll only have time to save our own skins and show little consideration for the other person.

5	In the end we'll not even really be friends – just people who know each other.	But underneath, love will have turned to hate, we'll be angry that we couldn't 'make it' and 'hit the jackpot'. Even though we've split up, we won't like our ex-partners seeing anyone else.
6	Just as children are frightened of falling through ice, having been hurt will make us cautious about getting emotionally involved with someone again.	But deep down, if we're absolutely honest, in time we wouldn't mind forgetting old wounds and becoming friends again at least.

This activity is replicated on Worksheet 3a in the online resources.

Activities E3 and E4 These activities are intended to invite students to justify their interpretation of a theme in the poem. Discussing the merits of each statement will reiterate the need to justify arguments and find evidence from the poem to support different views. Activity E4 will enable them to practise collating their views, formulating a coherent response and putting this into writing – which is an invaluable exam skill.

Evidence for all these statements can be found in the poem (see commentary in Activity E2).

Check your learning This activity is intended to reinforce what students have learned in this chapter and in the last activity, by explaining an image which the writer has extended.

'Match-makers' are people who try to arrange relationships (thus the name of the agency). The agency can do everything to ensure that two individuals are suitably matched except provide the chemical reaction or 'spark' that makes for a real love match. If you get too involved and get hurt, don't blame the agency – they only got you together!

Further reading

Other poems useful for studying imagery include:

- Norman MacCaig's 'Movements', a poem similar to (but more challenging than) 'Calendar', perhaps, in that it adopts a 'snapshot' approach to the description of a variety of creatures' appearance and movements, using a series of terse, memorable images. The poem uses some challenging vocabulary and has a thought-provoking conclusion, so may be better suited to Higher Tier students.

- Alan Ross's 'Night Patrol' is suitable for both tiers of student, but perhaps best used as a cloze exercise in mixed-ability groups. The poem is accessible in that it is purely descriptive; it uses an extensive series of images which are mainly visual. Used as a cloze exercise, different selections of omitted words could be used for different ability groups.

There are several poems which might be studied in connection with the 'Relationships' cluster in the Anthology, or specifically with 'The Thickness of Ice', as they each use extended metaphors to explore the nature of relationships between the sexes:

- Andrei Voznesensky's 'First Ice' is suitable for Foundation Tier students. In some anthologies you will find two drafts of the poem which students can compare.

- Seamus Heaney's 'Honeymoon Flight' and 'Scaffolding' each explore the theme of trust from different perspectives: both are suitable for both tiers of students.

- A stimulating poem also on the theme of love relationships which would challenge Higher Tier students is Seamus Heaney's 'Twice Shy', which develops a complex pattern of images.

Outcomes

In this chapter students have learned that:

- images can make you see, feel and think
- images can be extended to develop ideas.

AO focus

AO1: Respond to texts critically and imaginatively; select and evaluate relevant textual detail to illustrate and support interpretation.

AO2: Explain how language, structure and form contribute to writers' presentation of ideas, themes and settings.

In this chapter your students will:

- learn how poets organise their ideas and descriptions
- learn that poems often have a distinctive 'shape' that reinforces meaning.

Key terms

Key terms the students are introduced to in this chapter:

- Structure
- Pace
- Contrast
- Chronological

Poems included in this chapter

'Street Gang' by H Webster

The inclusion of this poem will please those teachers who think that too many literary texts presented to students are girl-friendly! Its content and language are accessible to all levels of ability. Much of the poem is descriptive, but the reflective conclusion, which is the focus of the activity, is thought-provoking.

'The Boys and Girls are Going Out to Play' by Dorothy Nimmo

Again, a suitable poem for study with mixed-ability groups. Its language is simple (it imitates the language of a nursery rhyme), but it contains subtle issues such as the poet's presentation of the girls' behaviour. Their behaviour is more admirable than the boys', on the surface, but the poet is uneasy about how unthinkingly they conform to a stereotype.

'Disabled' by Wilfred Owen

Another boy-friendly poem! This is a powerful but less frequently anthologised Owen poem, perfectly suitable for study by mixed-ability groups, provided that they are given sufficient input on the social/historical background (concepts such as 'esprit de corps', for instance), which is necessary anyway if students study the 'Conflict' cluster in the Anthology.

Wilfred Owen served in the army during the First World War. He was killed in battle just a week before the way ended in 1918.

'Night and Morning' by R S Thomas

The obvious use of contrast between the two stanzas of this short descriptive poem makes it ideal in enabling students of all abilities to show what they have learned about structure in this chapter.

Additional resources

PDF versions of all poems featured in the main text of this chapter are available for annotation purposes.

Audio recordings of some of the poems used in this chapter are also available in the online resources.

Getting started

In this chapter students learn how poets organise their writing in order to enhance meaning. In writing assignments on Shakespeare plays, students often find it difficult to comment effectively on structure, and yet if they focused on a series of scenes such as those at the opening of *Macbeth* and thought about the effects of contrasts in subject-matter, setting, mood, presentation of characters etc., they ought to be able to explain Shakespeare's dramatic purposes and techniques. In poetry, if students think about chronology/ development of ideas, contrast, and how stanzas are used as units of meaning, they will develop an understanding of how and why poems are organised.

Although structure has not been the focus of earlier chapters, it has been touched on in Chapters 1–3. Probably the best way of introducing this chapter is to revisit poems already studied and ask students to reflect on some of the following structural aspects of the poems:

- the patterned use of questions and development of the speaker's assertiveness in 'A Woman's Work' (Chapter 1)

- the movement from description to thoughts to final key idea in 'Night Nurses in the Morning' (Chapter 2)

- the shape of 'Calendar' and its neat organisation of the text into seasons (Chapter 3)

- the emphasis on chronological sequence in 'The Thickness of Ice' which results from the repetition of discourse markers at the openings of stanzas (Chapter 3).

Working through the chapter

A. A typical structure

Activity A1

Interactive activity: Effects of structure in 'O what is that sound' by W H Auden

Interactive activity: Responding to structure in 'An Irish Airman foresees his Death' by W B Yeats

This activity is intended to sharpen the focus of students' reading by looking below the surface of what is apparently straightforward description.

They are part of a gang and conform to its expectations. They find security in numbers. They have no clear idea of their personal identities, no clearly mapped purpose in life.

Activity A2 This activity is intended to encourage students to refine their thinking about the poet's intentions, and understand that the 'message' of a poem may be mainly implicit.

Statement 1: yes, this is true because 'none of them knows why', and the victim is a 'crucified scapegoat'.

Statement 2: this is implicit in the emphasis in the early stages of the poem on the description of the gang's boredom and lack of purpose. Also, the ending of the poem warns of the dangers if their violent behaviour should escalate.

Statement 3: the last three lines of the poem imply that the poet is suggesting otherwise.

Statement 4: referring to the comment on Statement 2, the reader might infer that the poet is less concerned with condemning the gang's behaviour than wishing that its energies could be channelled into more productive activities. There's also perhaps a sense that they are young and have the potential for change.

Another way of approaching this feature of structure in poetry is to ask students to explore poems which have significant endings, but delete the final key idea, 'moral' or 'message', and ask

them to write an ending which sums up/reflects the key idea in the poem. Then it is possible to discuss the actual ending and its impact – in, for example Seamus Heaney's 'Storm on the Island' or 'Follower'.

Activity A3 This activity looks at pace in the poem. Students are asked to look at how the poet has slowed down the pace at the beginning of the poem to reflect the gang's boredom by using incomplete sentences without verbs and lots of pauses. They are then asked to think about how the poet has increased the pace to reflect the energy of the attack. After the attack, the sentences are short and complete, the language is violent and forceful and there are more verbs.

B. Using contrast

Analysis activity: Exploring structure in 'The Convergence of the Twain' by Thomas Hardy

This part of the chapter examines the effect of contrast and also introduces the stanza as the most obvious organisational feature of poems.

Activity B1

Analysis activity: Exploring structure in 'Book Ends' by Tony Harrison

This activity is intended to heighten students' awareness of the effects of the shape of a poem on the printed page, here highlighting a central contrast.

Stereotyped views of the behaviour of boys and girls are represented in the descriptions below.

The boys

- Their imaginative play is violent (Stanza 2).

- They are destructive and single-minded, sweeping aside the natural world if it gets in their way (Stanza 4).

- They are violent and cruel towards each other (Stanza 6).

- They progress to more powerful bikes, and seem to be conforming to group peer expectations – 'Their helmets hide/their private faces' (Stanza 8).

- Their 'macho' behaviour is dangerous, and they end up having serious bike accidents (Stanza 10).

The girls

- They play imaginative games on the theme of domestic married bliss (Stanza 3).

- Their rides are on 'cuddly' animals, and they utilise aspects of the natural environment 'constructively' rather than destroy it (Stanza 5).

- They are emotional, domesticated and read romance fiction (Stanza 7).

- Following their romantic heroines, they conform to their mothers' expectations and get married (Stanza 9).

- They tackle their adult responsibilities and survive, but when they have children it is implied that they are merely perpetuating their own childhood in bringing them up; they are conforming to expectations (Stanza 11).

The contrast in the boys' and girls' behaviour is enhanced by the poem's structure. Once this has been established, you could 'cut and paste' the poem and match the parallel stanzas about aspects of the boys' and girls' behaviour in columns to highlight the contrasts.

Activity B2 This activity is intended to challenge students to think about implicit meaning – the thought that lies beneath the bald statement. Instigating a discussion here about the meaning of the last line should generate an interesting debate. This also reinforces the importance of final lines in poems and emphasises how they will often be used to sum up a poem's message.

Activity B3 This activity is intended to reinforce student's learning about the structure of the poem by focusing on its beginning, middle and end.

The poet's intentions are to:

Statement 1: 'set the scene'.

Statement 2: contrast the destructive aspects of the boys' behaviour with the constructive behaviour of the girls (is there an implicit contrast in the degrees of freedom experienced by the boys and girls, too?).

Statement 3: emphasise the inevitability of parents' realisation that they must eventually 'lose' their children. The line seems like a wistful acceptance that children will grow up and leave home.

Stretch yourself This activity is intended to provoke lively debate about a potentially contentious issue and encourage personal response from students. This poem raises some key questions about gender stereotypes and an exploration of this issue should enhance students' understanding and reinforce consideration of the poet's intentions.

In discussing the outcomes of the activities relating to 'The Boys and Girls are Going Out to Play', you might:

- identify the violent verbs used to describe the boys' behaviour

- study the positioning of words for emphasis at the beginnings of the second lines in the pairs of lines (enjambement), especially 'constructing', 'their private faces', 'pull through', 'their mothers' (note the emphasis – what do the girls think?), and 'to watch' (they are passive). Philip Larkin makes a similar observation in his poem 'Afternoons' about young mothers focusing on their parental responsibilities: 'Something is pushing them/To the side of their own lives'

- consider the deliberately extended 'punctuation spaces' either side of 'Or not.', which has an ominous tone.

- examine how rhyme emphasises the contrast of 'this is their proudest day' and 'They go the bravest way' ('bravest' being laced with irony)

- comment on the poem's rhyming pattern: the poem is presumably a parody of the nursery rhyme 'Boys and Girls Go out to Play'. It might be interesting to photocopy it and compare it with the poet's less idealised presentation of childhood here.

Ted Hughes' 'Jaguar' can also be used as an effective example of contrast. Here, the descriptions of the lazy and subdued animals serve to highlight the repressed energy and ferocity of the jaguar.

C. Out of order

Activity C1 This activity is intended to encourage students to think about the chronology of a poem.

As students will need to experiment with different stanza orders, they will do the exercise more effectively if you photocopy the 'scrambled' poem onto card and cut it up into stanzas so that students can move the stanzas around before finalising their chosen sequence.

'Disabled', in its correct order, appears at the end of the Student Book and also in the online resources.

Activity C2 This activity asks students to compare their chosen sequence with the original. It is intended to consolidate students' understanding of the poem's content and narrative sequence. The correct order is as follows:

Stanza 1: The boy is sitting in a wheelchair in an 'institute' – some form of hospital/care home – listening to the more active children playing. Students will have worked out the chronological disruption by now and may comment on it, so you might want to deal with the issue briefly before Activity C4.

Stanza 2: The boy is remembering the 'good times' before he went to war, when he socialised with girls.

Stanza 3: The poet emphasises how physically attractive the boy was. War seems to have aged him.

Stanza 4: He was good at sport and admired for his ability. He joined up when drunk, mainly to impress the girls (specifically Meg), who found military uniform attractive ('All the nice girls love a sailor/soldier').

Stanza 5: He didn't have any idea what he would be fighting for or what war was really like when he joined up. He had an idealised view and thought of the superficially attractive features of soldiering, not the horrors of war. Cynically, the recruitment officers 'turned a blind eye' to his lying about his age.

Stanza 6: His reception when he returned to England injured was a contrast with the happier receptions he used to receive from crowds after football matches.

Stanza 7: He is in the institution, helplessly waiting to be put to bed – where he was described in Stanza 1.

Sequencing exercises are effective activities in enabling students to explore structure. Poems which you might find useful to further illustrate this point include:

- Liz Lochhead's 'The Choosing'
- Marguerite Gazely's 'First Love'
- Wendy Cope's 'Tich Miller'
- Seamus Heaney's 'Mid-term Break'.

Activity C3   This activity is intended to help students to understand how the poet uses contrasts to move the reader to empathise with the tragic waste of the boy's potential.

Present and past sections will now be evident to students.

Statement 1: His natural handsomeness contrasts with his permanent disability and makes the reader more sympathetic. Would anyone think of painting him now?

Statement 2: The reader feels a sense of the tragedy of wasted potential – his sporting days are over.

Statement 3: Enlisting to impress the girls has gone tragically wrong. They were attracted by the superficial (his looks and uniform), and now they even avoid looking at him (Stanza 7), or touching him with affection (Stanza 2).

Statement 4: The reader feels anger that the boy was innocent and vulnerable, and that cynical adults who should have protected him were happy to see him used as 'cannon fodder'.

Activity C4   This activity is intended to focus students' reading on specific textual details in a long poem.

Stanza 2: He used to relish the company of girls and their physical attractions; now he is like a 'leper' to them. There is a powerful sense of regret at what now seems recklessness ('threw away his knees') and a terrible finality in 'Now, he will never feel again how slim/Girls' waists are' which contrast with the 'romantic' atmosphere created in the first three lines.

Stanza 3: He was once supremely handsome. Now he is physically 'broken', pallid, and prematurely old (a common motif in Owen's poetry). Again, 'Poured it down shell-holes' seems a bitter self-reproach for recklessness.

Stanza 4: Most of this stanza describes how the boy revelled in the attention of girls and how he thought of only the attractive aspects of military life. The simple but effective 'He wonders why.' undermines all these details; he had no important reason to enlist.

Activity C5   This activity is intended to emphasise the main purpose of studying the poem – to illustrate the powerful effect of disrupting chronological sequence to grab the reader's attention at the outset, and to explore how language is used to make the opening powerful.

- 'A wheeled chair' (not a 'wheelchair') emphasises his passivity.
- 'ghastly suit of grey' has overtones of 'ghostliness' and suggests impersonality.
- The 'mothered' image emphasises his dependence.
- 'saddening like a hymn' has a powerful melancholy.

Perhaps most effective is the positioning of 'Legless' at the opening of line 3, which comes as a shock to the reader.

Activity C6   is intended to illustrate to students that 'messages' in poems are not always explicit; instead of making statements, the poet uses questions.

The questions powerfully emphasise his helplessness and dependence on others. He has lost his independence as well as his limbs. The cold he feels may be more than physical.

You may wish to make links between the content/ themes of 'Disabled' and poems in the 'Conflict' cluster in the Anthology.

Check your learning

Viewpoints activity: 'Halley's Comet' by Stanley Kunitz

This activity is intended to reinforce what students have learned in the chapter about poets' use of contrast.

The poet writes two stanzas which contrast a scene in different weather conditions. In the first stanza he describes a savage storm, using words like 'blustered', and in the second he describes the calm after the storm, using gentler language like 'hush' and 'slumbered'. The lines in the two stanzas parallel each other very closely: lines 2 and 3 in each stanza focus on the beach and then the wind.

Further reading

Other poems useful for studying structure include:

- Seamus Heaney's 'Storm on the Island' and 'Mid-term Break'. These are good poems, especially for Foundation Tier students, to demonstrate how poems can develop towards a final 'message' or thought.

- Ted Hughes's 'The Jaguar' and Wilfred Owen's 'Dulce et Decorum Est'. These are sufficiently challenging to stretch Higher Tier students and are excellent poems to use to study structure. They are similar in that they begin with slow-paced general description of a scene, accelerate the pace when moving on to describe a specific creature/person, and have thought-provoking climaxes. The Owen poem is particularly good for demonstrating that the final philosophy, the ironic Latin motto, would not have the same impact if it had not been prepared by the graphic descriptions of the soldiers' suffering.

Outcomes

In this chapter students have learned that:

- the meaning and effects of poems can be enhanced by how poets organise their writing

- the stanza is an important feature of organisation in poems.

AO focus

AO1: Respond to texts critically and imaginatively; select and evaluate relevant textual detail to illustrate and support interpretation.

AO2: Explain how language, structure and form contribute to writers' presentation of ideas, themes and settings.

In this chapter your students will:

● learn how poets use word placement to reinforce effects of word choices

● learn some of the effects of rhyme and free verse.

Key terms

Key terms the students are introduced to in this chapter:

● Form

● Rhyme-scheme

● Rhythm

● Free verse

● Enjambement

● Prose

● Verse

Poems included in this chapter

'Another Christmas Poem' by Wendy Cope

As explained above, this is a very simple humorous rhyming poem.

Wendy Cope was born in 1945 and has won two major poetry awards. She is renowned for writing humorous poetry.

'Wires' by Philip Larkin

This is a more challenging poem, and students may need some help in grasping its core metaphor. Given that students find it difficult to write about rhyme, and that it isn't always evident why poets have chosen to write in rhyme, this is a useful poem to explore the effects of a deliberate choice of rhyme-scheme by the poet.

'Drummer Hodge' by Thomas Hardy

The poem should be accessible to all abilities of student, but explanation of context and vocabulary here are important – and students will be able to trace meaning more easily if there is some examination of the inversions of word-order (more typical of older styles of writing) used for deliberate effect. Students might like to think about how the second stanza might be rendered in modern 'prosaic' English, for instance.

Thomas Hardy was born in 1840 and died in 1928. He is one of the Victorian age's most famous poets and novelists.

'The Pond' by Owen Sheers

An accessible poem for all abilities of student, and more subtle than it appears on first reading. This is a particularly good example of the effects of free verse form.

'Living Space' by Imtiaz Dharker

Like many poems in this section of the book, this is a poem accessible because of its detailed description, but challenging because of the philosophy it develops in considering the subject of faith.

Imtiaz Dharker was born in Pakistan in 1954, but she was brought up in Glasgow.

Additional resources

PDF versions of all poems featured in this chapter are available for annotation purposes.

Audio recordings of some of the poems used in this chapter are also available in the online resources.

Getting started

In this chapter students learn how poets use verse form to emphasise key words and phrases. They consider the effects of rhyme and, in particular, how the flexibility of free verse enables poets to emphasise key words and phrases at the openings and endings of lines.

Verse form is a subject too wide ranging to cover in a short chapter of a textbook. Specific verse forms such as the sonnet might be more appropriately taught when students prepare relevant Anthology poems. Students often identify rhyme without then knowing what to say about it. The purpose of this chapter is to make them more aware that looking at where words are placed can help them to 'home in' on some of the most important ideas in a poem, and help them to write about why poets arrange lines as they do.

'Another Christmas Poem' is a useful starting point for looking at verse form, as it is a short and simple poem which introduces students to the accepted method of identifying rhyme. More importantly, it illustrates what will not be obvious to students – that the humour in the contrast of the two key phrases is enhanced by the rhyme – therefore highlighting word placement.

Rhyme is an important feature of the technique of deflation, commonly used in satire. An entertaining, more sustained poem to explore this with students is Charles Causley's 'The Ballad of the Bread Man'.

Working through the chapter

A. Poems that rhyme

🔊 Interactive activity: The best words for the best sounds

🔊 Interactive activity: Rhyme and rhythm in 'The Eagle' by Alfred, Lord Tennyson

Students are introduced here to the convention of labelling the ends of lines with letters to mark a poem's rhyme-scheme.

Activity A1 This activity is intended to help students to grasp the overall meaning of the poem.

Point 1: The cattle like to wander because, being young, they have the urge to explore the natural world around them; they have an inherent spirit of adventure, unlike old cattle, who have learned that they must not stray – they have encountered the shock of the electric fence as young cattle and their behaviour has been modified. Notice how "know" is contrasted with "scent"; the old cattle have learned from experience, the young cattle follow their instincts (see point 4).

Point 2: The young cattle have not learned the effects of electric fences, and they encounter them without warning ("blunder"). The power of the shock is vividly described: "muscle-shredding violence".

Points 3 and 4: The pain of the experience teaches the young cattle not to stray; they become like the old cattle. The last line implies that the cattle are artificially restricted from doing what they should naturally be allowed to do.

Activity A2 This activity is intended to help students to think about symbolism and to enhance their understanding of the poem's meaning by examining its central metaphor. Society has laws and codes of behaviour which prevent people from doing just what they want (and schools are a microcosm of society in this sense). People who break laws are punished; this teaches them how far they can safely challenge authority. Older people tend to grow more conservative; it is the idealistic young who rebel.

Activity A3 This activity is intended to help students to see that the rhyme scheme has a 'rebound' effect which mirrors the ideas in the poem.

It would seem artificial to plan to write a poem whose verse form mirrors its ideas as closely as here, but the rhyme structure does reflect the following pattern:

Outward journey of exploration – sudden shock of barrier – return to starting point.

However, the pattern does not seem contrived – it isn't immediately obvious, and the poem is beautifully crafted. There is a striking symmetry in the first three and last three lines, the opening and closing lines being neatly balanced. A case could be made for all three statements, but the second bullet point is the most interesting one to explore.

Activity A4 This activity is intended to encourage students to engage with the philosophical ideas of the poem and relate the ideas to aspects of their own lives.

All the statements are valid, of course, but have 'flip-sides'. These are interesting ideas stimulated by the poem which might lead, among other things, to a consideration of the reluctance of teachers to introduce young people to outdoor activities because of the culture of litigation (*The Lore and Language of Schoolchildren* by the Opies has an interesting chapter on dangerous games and the benefits to children of risk-taking).

Stretch yourself This activity is intended to reinforce what students have learned about use of contrast in Chapter 4 and it invites them to see that the word placement emphasises the juxtaposition – a prelude to the next section.

B. Word placement

🔊 Interactive activity: Rhyme and rhythm in 'Meeting at Night' by Robert Browning

🔊 Analysis activity: Exploring word placement in 'The song of Hiawatha' by Henry Wadsworth Longfellow

This part of the chapter introduces students to the significance of word placement, both within a line or stanza and within the poem as a whole. They are also introduced to the rhythm of a poem and its effect on interpretation.

Activities B1 and B2

(k) Interactive activity: Line placement in 'Anthem for Doomed Youth' by Wilfred Owen

These activities are intended to help students to understand clearly the particular structure and form of 'Drummer Hodge'.

Each stanza has the same rhyming structure, but the rhymes are different. The content of the three stanzas could be summed up as follows:

- Hodge's unceremonial burial in an alien country is described

- Hodge's youth and innocence – specifically about the cause of the war – is implied

- Hodge becomes assimilated in his new environment – he becomes part of the permanent natural world.

Activity B3 This activity is intended to help students to see that the impact of the phrases is created by the positioning as well as the choice of the words.

The poet wants the reader to see the burial as undignified and inhuman. Hodge is flung into the ground with nothing to mark his grave, as if worthless as a human being. At the beginning of the poem and at the beginnings of the lines, these words are emphatic, particularly 'uncoffined', because 'rest' at the end of line 1 creates a false sense of security, and does not prepare the reader for the bluntness of the word. As mentioned in the notes for Chapter 4, the poet's technique here is similar to that of Wilfred Owen's in his abrupt introduction of 'legless' at the opening of 'Disabled'.

Activity B4 This activity is intended to draw students' attention to an important clue to a change of emphasis/direction in the poem, and then to examine that development in detail.

'Yet' indicates a shift in emphasis; in the last stanza the tree becomes a sort of natural memorial, and there is a sense that he is at rest in this new environment, whereas he seemed estranged from his homeland in the first two stanzas.

Activity B5 This activity looks in detail at some of the imagery used by Hardy and the effect this has on the meaning of the poem.

In the first two stanzas the stars are 'foreign' and 'strange'; in the last stanza they are 'strange-eyed', but Hodge is finally in harmony with his new environment. The stars are 'His' (emphasised at the opening of the final line); they 'reign' majestically (stressed at end of the line), and they do so

'eternally', the guarantee of permanence ending the poem on a very positive note.

Activity B6 This activity is intended to practise the technique of writing critical comments in preparation for writing a full essay in the examination.

C. Free verse

(k) Viewpoints activity: 'Tall Nettles' by Edward Thomas

Activities C1 and C2 These activities are intended, as are many previous exercises, to encourage students to focus on the effects of significant details and their placement, this time through sample annotations.

Emphasised at the end of the line, 'Things' acquires a resonance as the poem develops – the 'things' are not objects, but important formative experiences in the speaker's childhood.

The alliteration helps emphasise these descriptive details, placed prominently at the openings of lines. The phrase 'sunk shallow' is visual, as is 'secret bruise' (a dark, round patch on a lighter background), but there is another layer of meaning in that a bruise might be kept secret not just because it is disfiguring, but because it might be the result of some experience the bearer didn't want to reveal. The phrase 'sucking squash' has a similar emphatic position and is made more forceful by its sound qualities (onomatopoeia). The 'shrinking carton' also has a strong visual impact.

The 'slug-lines' image conjures up an unattractive picture of congealed tears in meandering lines dried on the boy's cheeks.

As well as being emphatically positioned at the opening of the two lines, the juxtaposition of 'vowing never' and 'only to slink back' is highly effective because it emphasises the boy's volte-face, ironically explained in the last stanza – hunger and discomfort were stronger than principle! The fact that the latter phrase is a short complete line adds to the emphasis. The final line is beautifully balanced, the internal rhyme reinforcing the contrast of 'anger' and 'hunger'.

Enjambement is explained at this point and students are encouraged to think about the effect that this technique has rather than simply identifying it. Reading a poem aloud can help to make this device clear to students.

Activity C3 This activity reinforces the exploration of the placement of 'vowing' and 'slink back' in light of the learning about enjambement.

D. Prose into verse

Activities D1 and D2 These activities are intended to reinforce what students have learned about word placement in free verse poems, firstly in a creative task, and secondly by a discussion.

The poet has chosen a very flexible form of free verse, ending several sentences in the first stanza at the opening of lines to stress key ideas, for example 'straight lines', 'or parallel', 'balance', 'thrust', and 'Nails clutch'. The first stanza consists of a series of short, blunt statements, 'Nothing is flat' being emphasised in a short line on its own. The line 'The whole structure leans dangerously' draws attention to itself by its relative length, and the final line emphasises the precariousness of the building ('it'll be a miracle if it doesn't collapse') and prepares for the development of the theme of faith in the last stanza. There is an element of contradiction within lines in 'balance crookedly' and 'supports', and in 'Nails clutch' and 'open seams', which emphasises the idea of precariousness.

The second stanza gains emphasis from its relative brevity, the short final line underlining the poverty and insecurity of people's living conditions in this environment.

The last two stanzas, contrasting with the series of short sentences in the opening stanza, consist of a single sentence surging towards a climax which emphasises the importance of faith, symbolised by the eggs. They are as fragile as the buildings and as fragile as faith (note the emphatic placement of 'fragile curves'). 'The wire basket' they are contained in does not sound substantial, and 'hung out' makes them seem precariously placed. Is 'the dark edge/of a slanted universe' representative of a world that is socially as well as physically skewed? The opening word of 'gathering the light' is very positive, the light symbolising goodness and hope. The opening ends on a positive note, but the juxtaposition of 'bright' and 'thin' concludes the poem with a reminder that faith on the one hand offers hope but on the other is intangible and possibly frail.

The correct version of 'Living Space' appears at the back of the Student Book and also in the online resources.

To explore symbolism in greater depth, look at Robert Frost's poems 'Fire and Ice' and 'After Apple-picking'.

Activity D3 This activity will encourage students to think about the effect of a lack of rhyme-scheme on the meaning of a poem. This further develops their learning about the free verse form.

Check your learning

Analysis activity: Exploring rhyme and repetition in 'Do not go gentle into that good night' by Dylan Thomas

This activity is intended to give students the opportunity to demonstrate what they have learned in the chapter by analysing word order and positioning in a haiku poem.

This is a good example of a poet's use of inversion – changing the natural order of words to emphasise key words. The subject of the poem is held back until the final line to create a temporary mystery. 'Up' and 'goes' at the beginning and ending emphasise movement, and the repetition of 'Stitching' at the very centre of the poem reinforces the image by replicating the repetitive stitching movement.

Further reading

Other poems useful for studying verse form include:

- numerous contemporary poems which illustrate the effectiveness of free verse, including Theodore Roethke's 'Orchids' (a descriptive poem which uses varying lengths of line for effect), and Seamus Heaney poems such as 'Death of a Naturalist', 'Blackberry-picking' and 'Follower', which are suitable for both tiers of ability

- numerous poems which teachers will be familiar with from previous AQA anthologies which are written in free verse form but have very interesting individual patterns, for instance Grace Nichols' 'Island Man', Carol Ann Duffy's 'Valentine', Imtiaz Dharker's 'Blessing', and Lawrence Ferlinghetti's 'Two Scavengers in a Truck'. Students of both Foundation and Higher Tiers have written successfully about these poems in previous examinations.

Outcomes

In this chapter students have:

- learned how poets emphasise ideas by strategic word placement

- learned, in particular, some of the effects of rhyme and free verse.

Making your skills count in the exam: the Unseen question

AO focus

AO1: Respond to texts critically and imaginatively; select and evaluate relevant textual detail to illustrate and support interpretation.

AO2: Explain how language, structure and form contribute to writers' presentation of ideas, themes and settings.

In this chapter your students will:

- learn about what is required of them in the exam for Unit 2, Section B: Poetry across Time

- apply and practise their skills in order to respond to the exam question effectively.

About the exam

Structure and content of the exam

Unit 2, Section B: Poetry Across Time will be based on unseen poetry. Students will be provided with one poem that they will not have previously studied and they will answer one question in relation to it. There will be a different poem for Higher and Foundation Tiers. The question is worth 18 marks (12 per cent of their total GCSE mark) and candidates are advised to spend 30 minutes on this part of the paper.

In this Unit, candidates will take a skills-based approach to poetry in order to become engaged and critical readers. This means that they will be expected to respond to:

- ideas, themes and issues

- language (including sound and imagery), form and structure.

They will learn how to make informed, personal responses to poetry and to offer an interpretation of a poem which can be supported by textual evidence.

How to prepare candidates for the exam

(kt) Analysis activity: Analysing poems about parents and children

(kt) Analysis activity: Analysing sonnets

(kt) Analysis activity: Analysing animal poems

(kt) Analysis activity: Analysing voice in poems

Throughout their course of study, students should explore a range of poetry in order to practise their skills, formulate a coherent approach to analysis and build their confidence. The number of poems they should cover will be the equivalent of a complete cluster similar to those in the Anthology (approximately 15 poems). As students will only be studying one of the four Anthology clusters for the other section of the Unit 2 paper, 'practice' poems could be taken from the clusters that they are not directly exploring. Alternatively, students could study a selection of equivalent poems of your own choosing. It is suggested that you familiarise students with a range of poetic styles, themes and genres including sonnets, ballads and narratives, as they prepare for their exam.

Each of the chapters in Section A of the Student Book offers guidance on a different aspect of analysis and provides examples of some unfamiliar poems which students can explore. Students' confidence should improve as they work through this sustained approach so that they feel well equipped to analyse a poem they may never have seen before in an exam situation. You should encourage students to think about the key areas of analysis – meaning, language, imagery, structure and form – and to be confident in offering a personal response to poems. Remind students that their interpretations will be valid as long as they can be supported with evidence from the poem itself.

As indicated in the Student Book, success in this part of the examination will result not from a 'crash-course' revision assault, but by following an integrated programme of study which ensures that students have practised poetry reading skills throughout the two-year course. Revision should be a matter of reminding students of the key features to look for in a poem and referring them to relevant 'checklists', of revising such aspects of essay technique as effective use of quotations (for example, reminding them that as well as using quotations to back up points, they need to comment on the *effects* of quoted language on the reader), and practising writing under time pressure.

As the structure of examination questions will not vary from year to year, making up timed practice questions should not be difficult. Given that contextual notes are not provided in the examination, however, you need to choose poems without obscure 'details' – for example, Gillian Clarke's 'Neighbours', hastily selected from the 'Place' cluster of the Anthology, might not be suitable as students will need to know background details about the Chernobyl disaster in order to make an appropriate and informed response.

One of the problems with revision in English is that there is a limit to how many practice tests you can practically mark in the build-up to examinations. It is a good idea to encourage students to engage in peer assessment, and to discuss and match their individual efforts against 'model' answers. These could be answers you have written yourself, or student responses (such as the one in the Student Book) in the 'bank' you will eventually have created over time. Prior to timed tests, the paired revision activities recommended in the Student Book can be done in lessons, and you could extend paired activities by having pairs pass poems on to other pairs for further comment and annotation.

In the build-up to the examination, one way of checking that students are prepared is to ask them to create simple bullet-point style leaflets advising other GCSE students what to do and what not to do in the examination.

Remember that, once the examination has become established, there will be an annual Examiners' Report which you can access on the AQA website. Students often become blasé about meaningful advice from their teacher so it is helpful to 'go to the top' and find pertinent quotations which add further authority to your comments.

What students need to know

In the exam, students should be advised to:

- read the questions carefully
- think carefully before beginning to write
- underline key details in the text so that they are easy to find
- use quotations effectively
- comment on the effects of devices rather than merely spotting them
- allocate time appropriately within both the paper as a whole and any separate parts of one question
- check answers briefly (although this may be a luxury in a 30-minute answer).

Introducing the questions

The question that students will answer on the Unseen poetry element of the Unit 2 question will be structured differently according to the tier for which they have been entered.

Foundation Tier

Students will be provided with a different poem from the Higher students and they must answer the single question given. This question will be broken down into two parts: part (a) will ask students to consider *what* the poet wishes to express and part (b) will ask students to comment on *how* the poet expresses their view. Any difficult vocabulary will be defined on the paper. Although the question is divided into parts, students' answers will not be given separate marks, but a combined mark out of 18.

So for instance, a Foundation Tier unseen question might look like the following:

> Answer **both** parts (a) and (b).
>
> Part (a)
>
> What do you think the speaker feels about his son in this poem?
>
> **and**
>
> Part (b)
>
> How does the poet present his feelings about his son by the ways he describes him?
>
> (*18 marks*)

Higher Tier

Students will be provided with a poem and they must answer the single question given. This question will ask students to consider *what* the poet is saying about a certain idea or issue and *how* the poet is presenting this view. Students will be awarded a mark out of 18.

So for instance, a Higher Tier unseen question might look like the following:

> 1 What do you think the poet is saying about the ways that some people deal with the breakdown of a relationship? How does he present his ideas? (*18 marks*)

Practice exam questions
- Planning activity: 'Nettles'
- Planning activity: 'Bayonet Charge'
- On your marks activity: 'Granny Scarecrow'

Students are provided with sample exam questions for both Higher and Foundation Tier in the Student Book.

Outcomes

In this chapter students have learned how to:

- prepare for Section B of Unit 2 of the exam
- write a comprehensive response to the question set.

Section B: Poetry from the Anthology

Introduction

The Section opener in the Student Book explains to students what they will be required to do in the exam for the Anthology question and it states how this Section will help them to prepare. It is important that students understand that the skills they developed in Section A should also now be used in Section B. Furthermore, the Section opener outlines how the poems in the Anthology are organised into clusters by a common theme: 'Characters and voices', 'Place', 'Conflict' and 'Relationships'. Students should clearly understand that they only study one cluster of poems (15 poems) and that they answer the exam question related to that particular cluster. The Section contains a chapter on each of the four clusters of poetry. Each chapter looks at six poems – a mixture from contemporary and Literary Heritage – from that cluster. The rest of the poems in the clusters are covered in the accompanying online resources.

As well as investigating meaning, language and imagery, structure and form, and students' own personal responses, the chapters provide background information about the poets and their poems, as well as some explanation as to why each poem has been included in the cluster and how it relates to the broader theme.

Assessment Objectives

There are three Assessment Objectives for this part of the paper:

AO1: Respond to texts critically and imaginatively; select and evaluate relevant textual detail to illustrate and support interpretation.

AO2: Explain how language, structure and form contribute to writers' presentation of ideas, themes and settings.

AO3: Make comparisons and explain links between texts, evaluating writers' different ways of expressing meaning and achieving effects.

It is obviously important that students understand what they will be assessed on in the exam and therefore it may be more helpful to share the Assessment Objectives in a student-friendly way. Students may use the following bullet points as a checklist for the unit as a whole:

- I can express a personal response.
- I can locate and select relevant quotations to support my interpretation.
- I can explain and evaluate the quotations I have selected.
- I can explain how a poet has used language and structure and I understand the effects these may have on the reader.
- I can analyse the themes and ideas that are presented by the poets.
- I can make comparisons and contrasts between the poems in the cluster that I am studying.

Approaches to analysing Anthology poetry

Here are a few generic ideas on how to approach the Anthology poetry:

- Sequencing – divide the poem up into sections and ask the students to assemble the poem in what they think is the original form. Discuss different responses with them and ask them how they decided on the sequence they chose; for example did a narrative or a rhyme pattern guide them?
- Show students a selection of pictures and ask them to identify quotations which depict the images.
- Ask students to generate questions that they want to ask about the poem.
- Create a series of 'True or False' or 'Odd One Out' questions to help students to access the text. These activities can also be used to review learning.
- A jigsaw approach does not allow any student to be passive in a lesson. Initially, students work in expert groups on a particular section of a poem, for example one stanza. They may be given prompts to aid their analysis but they have to annotate their stanza and be prepared to feed back on it.
Next, the groups are changed so that one person working on each stanza now forms a new group and

they take it in turns to explain their stanza to the other members of their new group. By the end, all students will have the full poem annotated and the teacher has only acted as a facilitator for the learning.

● PEE grids (Point, Evidence, Explanation) can help pupils to structure their analysis. Hand out partly-completed grids into which students have to locate a quotation to match a point and explanation, or into which they have to write an explanation for a quotation that has been supplied.

● When students are working on comparing the poems, tables such as the following can help to structure their thoughts:

	Poem 1	Poem 2
Attitudes and ideas		
Language and imagery		
Structure and form		

Remind students that it is important that they recognise and comment on differences as well as similarities.

Nelson Thornes resources

Chapter	Student Book poems and activities	(k!) resources
7. Characters and voices	**Characters and voices** Generating ideas about narrative voice and its effects **'Checking out me history' by John Agard** 1–5: Analysing and commenting on meaning; explaining the poem in historical and cultural terms 6–7: Analysing and commenting on language and imagery 8–9: Analysing and commenting on structure and form 10: Developing a personal response **'Horse Whisperer' by Andrew Forster** 1–7: Analysing and commenting on meaning 8–11: Analysing and commenting on language and imagery 12–13: Analysing and commenting on structure and form 14–15: Developing a personal response **'My Last Duchess' by Robert Browning** 1–7: Analysing and commenting on meaning Stretch yourself: Explaining the social context – the impact of the nobility in the Victorian era 8–9: Analysing and commenting on language and imagery 10–11: Analysing and commenting on structure and form 12: Developing a personal response **'The Ruined Maid' by Thomas Hardy** 1–4: Analysing and commenting on meaning Stretch yourself: Writing a dialogue based on the poem 5: Analysing and commenting on language and imagery 6–9: Analysing and commenting on structure and form 10: Developing a personal response **'Brendon Gallacher' by Jackie Kay** 1–5: Analysing and commenting on meaning 6–8: Analysing and commenting on language and imagery 9–10: Analysing and commenting on structure and form Stretch yourself: Rewriting the poem as a short story 11: Developing a personal response **'On a Portrait of a Deaf Man' by John Betjeman** 1–3: Analysing and commenting on meaning Stretch yourself: empathising with the poet's point of view 4–5: Analysing and commenting on language and imagery 6–7: Analysing and commenting on structure and form 8: Developing a personal response **Comparing poems** 1–5: Practising writing a comparative essay	Interactive activity: 'Medusa' by Carol Ann Duffy Interactive activity: 'Give' by Simon Armitage Interactive activity: 'Les Grands Seigneurs' by Dorothy Molloy Analysis activity: 'Singh Song' by Daljit Nagra Interactive activity: 'Case history: Alison (head injury)' by U A Fanthorpe Interactive activity: Responding to 'Horse Whisperer' Interactive activity: 'On a Portrait of a Deaf Man' by John Betjeman Analysis activity: Comparing 'The Clown Punk' and 'Ozymandias' Analysis activity: Comparing 'My Last Duchess' and 'The Ruined Maid' Viewpoints activity: Comparing 'The River God' and 'My Last Duchess' Planning activity: Comparing poems from 'Characters and voices' Planning activity: Comparing two poems of your choice from the cluster Worksheet 7a: 'checking out me history', Activity 2 Worksheet 7b: 'Horse Whisperer', Activity 1 Worksheet 7c: 'Horse Whisperer', Activity 2 Worksheet 7d: 'The Ruined Maid', Activity 2 Worksheet 7e: 'On a Portrait of a Deaf Man', Activity 2 Worksheet 7f: Choosing your comparison poem Audio recordings of a selection of the poems

Chapter	Student Book poems and activities	**k!** resources
8. Place	**Place** Reflecting on the importance of places **'Cold Knap Lake' by Gillian Clarke** 1–2: Analysing and commenting on meaning 3–4: Analysing and commenting on language and imagery 5–7: Analysing and commenting on structure and form Stretch yourself: Explaining the contrast between a physical and a mental or emotional place 8: Developing a personal response **'The Wild Swans at Coole' by W B Yeats** 1–3: Analysing and commenting on meaning 4–5: Analysing and commenting on language and imagery 6–8: Analysing and commenting on structure and form 9–10: Developing a personal response Stretch yourself: Explaining the impact of the poet's view about love **'London' by William Blake** 1–2: Analysing and commenting on meaning; explaining the impact of historical context 3–6: Analysing and commenting on language and imagery 7–8: Analysing and commenting on structure and form 9: Developing a personal response Stretch yourself: Altering the tone of the poem **'Spellbound' by Emily Brontë** 1–2: Analysing and commenting on meaning 3–6: Analysing and commenting on language and imagery 7–10: Analysing and commenting on structure and form 11–12: Developing a personal response **'Wind' by Ted Hughes** 1–2: Analysing and commenting on meaning 3–5: Analysing and commenting on language and imagery 6–7: Analysing and commenting on structure and form Stretch yourself: Explaining the poet's views on man and nature 8: Developing a personal response **'Neighbours' by Gillian Clarke** 1–2: Analysing and commenting on meaning 3–8: Analysing and commenting on language and imagery 9–11: Analysing and commenting on structure and form Stretch yourself: Close reading of the use of the word 'neighbour' and its meaning in the poem 12: Developing a personal response **Comparing poems** 1–5: Practising writing a comparative essay	Interactive activity: Vocabulary in 'Below the Green Corrie' Interactive activity: Responding to 'A Vision' by Simon Armitage Viewpoints activity: Understanding 'The Moment' by Margaret Atwood Analysis activity: A close look at 'The Blackbird of Glanmore' Interactive activity: 'Price We Pay for the Sun' by Grace Nichols Interactive activity: Responding to 'Hard Water' by Jean Sprackland Analysis activity: A close look at 'The Prelude' Analysis activity: Analysing 'Storm in the Black Forest' by D H Lawrence Planning activity: Comparing MacCaig and Wordsworth Interactive activity: Reflecting on the 'Place' cluster Worksheet 8a: Introductory activity Worksheet 8b: 'The Wild Swans at Coole', Activity 1 Worksheet 8c: 'London', Activity 1 Worksheet 8d: 'Wind', Activity 1 Worksheet 8e: 'Wind', Activity 2b Worksheet 8f: Choosing your comparison poem Audio recordings of a selection of the poems
9. Conflict	**Conflict** Reflecting on different types of conflict **'Flag' by John Agard** 1–3: Analysing and commenting on meaning 4–7: Analysing and commenting on language and imagery 8–11: Analysing and commenting on structure and form 12: Developing a personal response **'Futility' by Wilfred Owen** 1–5: Analysing and commenting on meaning 6–7: Analysing and commenting on language and imagery 8–9: Analysing and commenting on structure and form 10: Developing a personal response	Analysis activity: 'You have picked me out' Viewpoints activity: 'The Yellow Palm' Interactive activity: Responding to 'The Right Word' Interactive activity: 'Falling Leaves' Interactive activity: 'Come on, come back' Interactive activity: Responding to 'Bayonet Charge'

Chapter	Student Book poems and activities	(k!) resources
9. Conflict *continued*	**'Mametz Wood' by Owen Sheers** 1–3: Analysing and commenting on meaning Stretch yourself: Writing a newspaper article based on the poem 4–5: Analysing and commenting on language and imagery 6–7: Analysing and commenting on structure and form 8–9: Developing a personal response **'The Charge of the Light Brigade' by Alfred, Lord Tennyson** 1–3: Analysing and commenting on meaning Stretch yourself: Writing from the point of view of one of the soldiers 4–6: Analysing and commenting on language and imagery 7–8: Analysing and commenting on structure and form 9: Developing a personal response **'Belfast Confetti' by Ciaran Carson** 1–4: Analysing and commenting on meaning Stretch yourself: Writing an eye witness account 5–7: Analysing and commenting on language and imagery 8–11: Analysing and commenting on structure and form 12: Developing a personal response **'Hawk Roosting' by Ted Hughes** 1–4: Analysing and commenting on meaning 5–6: Analysing and commenting on language and imagery 7–9: Analysing and commenting on structure and form 10–11: Developing a personal response Stretch yourself: Writing a poem based on 'Hawk Roosting' **Comparing poems** 1–5: Practising writing a comparative essay	Analysis activity: 'next to god of course america' Viewpoints activity: Comparing 'At the border' with 'Cameo Appearance' Analysis activity: Comparing your choice of poems Interactive activity: Multiple choice quiz on 'Conflict' cluster Worksheet 9a: 'Futility', Activity 3 Worksheet 9b: 'The Charge of the Light Brigade', Activity 2 Worksheet 9c: Choosing your comparison poem Audio recordings of a selection of the poems included
10. Relationships	**Relationships** Reflecting on own relationships **'Nettles' by Vernon Scannell** 1–4: Analysing and commenting on meaning 5–8: Analysing and commenting on language and imagery 9–11: Analysing and commenting on structure and form 12: Developing a personal response Stretch yourself: Analysing the poet's views on poetry **'Praise Song for my Mother' by Grace Nichols** 1–4: Analysing and commenting on meaning 5–6: Analysing and commenting on language and imagery 7–9: Analysing and commenting on structure and form 10–11: Developing a personal response Stretch yourself: Writing a praise song **'How do I Love Thee?' by Elizabeth Barrett Browning** 1–2: Analysing and commenting on meaning 3–4: Analysing and commenting on language and imagery 5–7: Analysing and commenting on structure and form Stretch yourself: Analysing the use of repetition in the poem 8: Developing a personal response	Interactive activity: 'Ghazal' by Mimi Khalvati Interactive activity: Responding to 'The Engine' by Jean Sprackland Interactive activity: Responding to 'In Paris With You' by James Fenton Viewpoints activity: 'Harmonium' by Simon Armitage Analysis activity: Analysing 'Hour' by Carol Ann Duffy Interactive activity: Interpreting 'Let me not unto the marriage of true minds' by William Shakespeare Analysis activity: Analysing 'Born Yesterday' by Philip Larkin Viewpoints activity: 'The Farmer's Bride' by Charlotte Mew Analysis activity: Exploring 'Nettles' by Vernon Scannell

Chapter	Student Book poems and activities	_k!_ resources
10. Relationships _continued_	**'To His Coy Mistress' by Andrew Marvell** 1–2: Analysing and commenting on meaning Stretch yourself: Explaining the impact of social and historical context on the tone of the poem 4–6: Analysing and commenting on language and imagery 7: Analysing and commenting on structure and form 8: Developing a personal response **'The Manhunt' by Simon Armitage** 1–3: Analysing and commenting on meaning 4–6: Analysing and commenting on language and imagery 7–9: Analysing and commenting on structure and form 10: Developing a personal response **'Quickdraw' by Carol Ann Duffy** 1–4: Analysing and commenting on meaning 5–9: Analysing and commenting on language and imagery 10–12: Analysing and commenting on structure and form 13: Developing a personal response **Comparing Poems** 1–5: Practising writing a comparative essay	Planning activity: Comparing Rossetti and Mew Interactive activity: Examining the form of some of the poems in the 'Relationships' cluster Worksheet 10a: 'How Do I Love Thee?', Activity 1 Worksheet 10b: 'To His Coy Mistress', Activity 3 Worksheet 10c: 'The Manhunt', Activity 2 Worksheet 10d: 'Quickdraw', Activity 2 Worksheet 10e: Choosing your comparison poem Audio recordings of a selection of the poems included
11. Making your skills count in the exam – the Anthology question	Analysing sample example questions, student responses and examiner comments	Planning activity: 'Characters and voices' On your marks activity: 'Place' On your marks activity: 'Conflict' Worksheet 11a: 'Conflict' Worksheet 11b: Comparing poems in the 'Relationships' cluster
12. Making your skills count in the controlled assessment	Analysing sample example questions, student responses and teacher comments 1–2: Selecting a comparison poem	Planning activity: Genre and form

7 Characters and voices

AO focus

AO1: Respond to texts critically and imaginatively; select and evaluate relevant textual detail to illustrate and support interpretation.

AO2: Explain how language, structure and form contribute to writers' presentation of ideas, themes and settings.

AO3: Make comparisons and explain links between texts, evaluating writers' different ways of expressing meaning and achieving effects.

In this chapter your students will:

- explore the theme of character and voice in poetry
- analyse and comment on the meaning, language, imagery, structure and form of a selection of poems from the 'Characters and voices' cluster of their Anthology through close reading and investigation activities
- explain poems in relation to social, cultural and historical settings
- strengthen their own understanding and use of poetic terms
- gain confidence in making a personal response to the poems they read.

In the course of the chapter, students analyse a sample selection of the poems from the 'Characters and voices' cluster of the Anthology. The key aspects of analysis that students covered in Section A of the Student Book: meaning (Chapter 1), language (Chapter 2), imagery (Chapter 3), structure (Chapter 4) and verse form (Chapter 5), now shape the progression of activities in Section B, so that for each poem in turn, students are asked to answer questions on meaning, language and imagery, structure and form, and personal response. The addition of personal response here reflects the need for students to engage with texts on an individual level – something examiners will be looking for evidence of. It is hoped that this consistent and logical approach will help to demystify the study of poetry and increase students' confidence by equipping them with a clear method with which to apply their skills of analysis.

Key terms

Key terms the students are introduced to in this chapter:

- Autobiographical
- Persona
- First person narration
- Third person narration
- Accent
- Dialect
- Standard English
- Dramatic monologue
- First person pronoun
- Possessive pronoun
- Couplets
- Dialogue
- Quatrain
- Refrain

Poems included in this chapter

Six of the poems from this cluster are covered in the Student Book, the remainder are covered in the online resources. The poems covered in the Student Book are written by male and female poets, both contemporary and from the English Literary Heritage. Most of the poems in this chapter are suitable for students studying both Foundation and Higher Tiers, with the exception of 'The Ruined Maid' and 'Brendon Gallacher' which are suitable for Foundation students.

Poems covered in this chapter:

- 'checking out me history' by John Agard
- 'Horse Whisperer' by Andrew Forster
- 'My Last Duchess' by Robert Browning
- 'The Ruined Maid' by Thomas Hardy
- 'Brendon Gallacher' by Jackie Kay
- 'On a Portrait of a Deaf Man' by John Betjeman

Poems from 'Characters and voices' covered by online resources:

- **kt** Interactive activity: Carol Ann Duffy's 'Medusa'
- **kt** Interactive activity: Simon Armitage's 'Give'
- **kt** Interactive activity: Dorothy Molloy's 'Les Grands Seigneurs'
- **kt** Analysis activity: 'Singh Song' by Daljit Nagra
- **kt** Interactive activity: 'Case history: Alison (head injury)' by U A Fanthorpe

Additional resources

Worksheets:

- 7a: 'checking out me history' Activity 2
- 7b: 'Horse Whisperer' Activity 1
- 7c: 'Horse Whisperer' Activity 2
- 7d: 'The Ruined Maid' Activity 2
- 7e: 'On a Portrait of a Deaf Man' Activity 2
- Choosing your comparison poem

Audio recordings of some of the poems used in this chapter are also available in the online resources, including some alternative readings.

Getting started

The theme of characters and voices is introduced here to encourage students to think about why this is an area that poets choose to write on. They are invited to consider whether the voice a poet chooses is autobiographical or the assumed voice of a persona. They are introduced to the different forms of narration poets can adopt in order to express the feelings and motivations of the characters they create. The different effects that first and third person narration can have on a reader's interpretation of a character are also introduced here. The poems that are covered in this chapter explore a range of characterisation; from Browning's possessive persona in 'My Last Duchess' to Betjeman's bittersweet tribute to his father in 'On a Portrait of a Deaf Man'. At the beginning of the activities for each poem, the theme of characters and voices is reinforced and students are encouraged to think about why each particular poem appears in this cluster and what it has to offer in an exploration of this theme.

Throughout the chapter, students are reminded that they should always consider the theme of this cluster and think about what the individual poets are saying about characters and voices in each of the poems. The activities, therefore, continually link back to this theme while exploring different aspects of analysis.

Activity This introductory activity is intended to help students get to grips with first and third person narration and to see the different effects these forms of narration can have on a reader's interpretation of a character. Students should notice how much closer a reader can feel to a character's thoughts and feelings when they are written in the first person.

Working through the chapter

Background information is given for each of the six poems in this chapter. Some biographical information is given about each poet and some introductory information about each poem is provided so that students can contextualise poems before embarking on a full analysis.

Of course, you may not have time in the classroom to explore each of the poems in the cluster in as much detail as is explored in the Student Book. The material that is presented here is intended as a suggested 'ideal' model of approach but you may only be able to select certain areas to focus on. It is hoped that you will be able to apply some, if not all, of this approach – however, it is by no means prescriptive and should not be interpreted as the number of activities that students will 'need' to have completed in preparation for their exam.

The personal response activities are crucial but by their nature are problematic to assess. For these activities, some guidance regarding the sort of response students are likely to submit is given, but this should by no means be taken as 'correct'. Students should be encouraged to engage with the poems on a personal level and to feel confident in voicing their interpretations as long as they can be supported with evidence from the poem text.

Before the poems are looked at in detail, students could be reminded of the guidance on how to read a poem, guidance they met in the Section A introduction. This summarises all the key areas that they should pay attention to as they read the Anthology poems for the first time.

'checking out me history' by John Agard

This poem is suitable for students entered for both Foundation and Higher Tiers. It presents Agard's desire to learn more about his cultural heritage.

Meaning

Activity 1 This activity is intended to help students feel confident discussing the poem's content by asking them to research the terms they are unfamiliar with.

You could ask groups of students to look up images on the internet of some of the figures Agard mentions to help them visualise the culture. Groups could present a term they have researched to the class.

Activity 2 This activity is intended to help students to see the contrast between what Agard learns and what else he wants to learn. The table could be completed as follows:

What he was taught	Other things he wanted to be taught
1066 – The Battle of Hastings/Dick Whittington	Toussaint L'Ouverture
The man who discovered the balloon and the cow who jumped over the moon/the dish that ran away with the spoon	Nanny de Maroon
Lord Nelson and Waterloo	Shaka the Zulu
Columbus and 1492	The Caribs and the Arawaks
Florence Nightingale and the lamp/Robin Hood/King Cole	Mary Seacole

This activity is replicated on Worksheet 7a in the online resources.

Activity 3 This activity asks students to study an annotation of the text.

a Students should be making the point that Agard thinks it is important to study a range of historical events to help people make sense of their identity and history. 'Blind me to me own identity' shows that he feels he has not been taught about his own Caribbean heritage; he has only been taught British history.

b Agard is afraid that he will lose his Caribbean heritage which contributes towards his identity. He does not want the history of the Caribbean (for example the people he names) to be lost. He wants to understand where he has come from.

Activity 4 This activity requires students to consider Agard's feelings about his identity.

The poet feels angry that his identity cannot be complete as he has not been told about Caribbean history. The tone is almost sarcastic when he states that he has been told about fictional figures such as King Cole and Dick Whittington but heroes such as Nanny de Maroon have been ignored. He is determined to put this right which is why he uses the poem to inform others about great figures in Caribbean history. He is 'checking out' his history/identity for himself. Any of the words given can be supported by evidence from the poem.

Activity 5 This activity asks students to think about the poem's final line.

Agard is informing the reader that he will not tolerate the lack of teaching about his Caribbean heritage. Instead, he is proactive in researching the history he wants to discover. The word 'carving' is forceful and suggests that he is reconstructing the heritage that has been hidden from him. The prominent placing of this line at the close of the poem highlights its significance.

Students are reminded that they looked at the significance of final lines in Chapter 4.

Language and imagery

Activity 6 This activity introduces students to accent, dialect and Standard English. You may wish to hold some general discussion about these linguistic terms to ensure all students understand their significance in terms of characterisation before moving on.

a Some suggestions of Agard's dialect are:

- 'wha' – what
- 'fo' – to
- 'me' – my
- 'bout' – about
- 'dat' – that
- 'de' – the

Some students may also want to explore the grammatical differences, for example how suffixes are absent ('happen' not 'happened') and how some words are missing from sentences.

b Agard is complaining in the poem that his Caribbean heritage has been omitted from his education and therefore he feels part of his identity is absent. By writing in his dialect he is highlighting his Caribbean roots and revealing another element of his identity that is strong. It also adds authenticity to the voice in the poem and strengthens his argument.

Activity 7 This activity asks students to look at repetition in the poem.

Agard repeats 'dem tell me' to emphasise that he was told a great deal but it wasn't always relevant to him. Notice how what he was told is always a longer list. He feels his identity is incomplete.

Structure and form

Activity 8 This activity requires students to consider a list of possible interpretations of some lines.

Students could be encouraged to see how these stanzas contain some of the history that he feels has been ignored and so wants the information to stand out.

Activity 9 This activity asks students to consider the lack of punctuation in the poem.

Students could choose from multiple examples and should write a succinct sentence about how this demonstrates Agard's ferocious determination to learn more about his heritage. Students could also suggest that the lack of pauses emphasises the flowing nature of history which is constantly moving and evolving.

Personal response

Activity 10   This activity requires a personal response from students.

You could collate responses from students and write them on the board.

'Horse Whisperer' by Andrew Forster

Interactive activity: Responding to 'Horse Whisperer'

This poem is suitable for students entered for both Foundation and Higher Tiers. It explores the change in attitude towards the work of horse whisperers'.

Meaning

Activity 1   This activity is intended to help students think about the role of horse whisperers before they commence their analysis.

This activity requires a personal response from students and should help them to practise formulating pertinent questions to aid their analysis.

This activity is replicated on Worksheet 7b in the online resources.

Activity 2   This activity asks students to closely study the poem's content and will help to impress the importance of backing up comments with evidence from the poem. The table could be completed as follows:

Evidence	Comment
'They shouted for me'	The repetition shows that horse whisperers were much sought after at one time. Farmers believed they could cure a variety of problems.
'a new fear to fight the fear of fire'	The alliteration and repetition of 'fear' give this line importance. It refers to the frog's wishbone which was believed to be the whisperers' most important charm. Many believed it bewitched the horses. There is a spell-like quality in this line.
'I swore I would protect/this legacy of whispers'	Whisperers wanted to keep their charms/gifts secret to secure their employment.
'I was the life-blood/no longer'	As farming technology developed, the demand for horse whisperers fell.
'the tractor came over the fields/like a warning.'	The simile is poignant as it is indicating how whisperers were no longer needed as horses were replaced by tractors. The word 'warning' is important as it is linked to danger and the whisperers were driven out of villages with pitchforks.
'Still I miss them.'	This mourns the loss of the relationship between the horses and the whisperers.

This activity is replicated on Worksheet 7c in the online resources.

Activity 3   This activity requires students to closely read the poem and pick out details of the horse whisperer's work.

Horse whisperers were much sought after as farmers often believed that they could cure any agitated horse. Examples of when farmers called for whisperers in the poem are when:

* horses snorted
* horses were restless: 'restless hooves traced circles in the earth'
* horses wouldn't pull the plough: 'shimmering muscles refused the plough'
* horses reared at fire: 'reared at burning straw'
* horses' eyes 'revolved'.

The wide range of reasons illustrates the importance at one time of the horse whisperer's trade.

Activity 4   This activity focuses students' attention on one key line of the poem.

The line indicates how important the whisperer once was to the farmer – the 'life-blood'. Farmers relied upon the whisperer's healing powers. However, as horses were replaced by tractors, the whisperers became redundant and the farmers turned against them. They were important 'no longer'.

Activity 5   This activity asks students to analyse the content of the poem.

The whisperers got their revenge by placing 'A foul hex above a stable door'. This spell aimed to make horses unrideable.

Activity 6   This activity asks students to consider the type of narration employed by Forster.

One example is: 'I was scorned as demon and witch.'

a   The use of the first person places the reader closer to the plight of the horse whisperers and we feel greater pity for them. We are sympathetic towards them and not the farmers.

b   Explore with students that 'me' could represent the voice of many horse whisperers who were treated in this way.

Activity 7   This activity asks students to revisit Activity 1 and complete the table in light of what they have learned about horse whisperers from the poem.

This will help them to visualise the progress of their analysis and learning.

Language and imagery

Activity 8 This activity focuses students' attention on Forster's use of metaphor.

The metaphor 'tender giants' reflects the size and sweet nature of the horses. It reveals the respect that the whisperers had for the horses.

Activity 9 This activity draws students' attention to a simile in the poem.

Forster is suggesting how effective the charms of the whisperers were and how the horses were powerless and needed help which only the horse whisperer could provide. It makes the whisperers sound dominant and hints that their work was relatively easy for them.

Activity 10 This activity asks students to consider Forster's use of language.

Forster communicates the beauty of the horses by explaining how the whisperers miss the horses. The descriptions also show respect and beauty: 'searing breath, glistening veins,/steady tread and the pride'. He creates a sense of majesty about the horses.

Activity 11 This activity asks students to examine the tone of the poem.

The tone of the poem is very mixed. It starts full of pride as the whisperer explains his skills and role. However, when we discover how the whisperers were treated when tractors were introduced, the tone becomes bitter and sorrowful. The ending is quite sad as the whisperer remembers the horses with fondness and laments the loss of the relationship between horse and whisperer.

Structure and form

Activity 12 This activity asks students to select a reason for Forster's use of repetition.

Students should be directed towards the second bullet point.

Activity 13 This activity focuses students' attention on the length of the lines in the poem.

The lines in the last stanza could be shorter to indicate that the regard that the horse whisperers were held in diminished over the years as their role became less useful.

Personal response

Activity 14 This activity requires a personal response from students.

Students may feel sorry for the horse whisperers or they may be sceptical of their practices. Ask students to explain why they feel the way they do.

Activity 15 This activity also requires a personal response from students.

You could ask pairs to share their questions with the class and encourage other pairs to offer potential responses.

'My Last Duchess' by Robert Browning

This poem is suitable for students entered for both Foundation and Higher Tiers. It is written as a dramatic monologue in which the Duke discusses his former wife.

Meaning

Activity 1 This activity asks students to think about how this poem fits the form of the dramatic monologue.

For students to access this question, you will need to have looked into the term 'dramatic monologue'. Students should validate any responses with exemplification from the text, such as first person narrative: 'and **I** chose never to stoop'. In pairs, students could track through the poem, discussing what he reveals about his past, present and future in progressive stages of his monologue.

Activity 2 This activity asks students to consider the relationship between the Duke and Duchess and to think about what this tells the reader about the Duke's character.

a Allow students to close read all references to the Duke and Duchess's relationship, highlighting that it appeared to be one based on distrust, envy and jealousy.

b This part of the activity requires personal and varied responses. Students should be able to support any of the following: sinister, jealous, possessive. Below is an example of one such response:

  • Sinister: 'half flush that dies along her throat' (line 19) and 'I gave commands' (line 45).

Activity 3 This activity focuses students' attention on the fact that the Duke never refers to his last wife by her first name.

Examples will include: 'my last Duchess', 'she' and 'her'. Take valid responses from the students as to why the Duke never refers to her by her name. Students might argue that this reinforces the fact that to him she was a possession, something that could be discarded. He removes her identity as a separate person in her own right by refusing to refer to her by her name.

Activity 4 This activity draws students' attention to the repeated first person and possessive pronouns.

Before responding to this question, encourage the students to highlight all examples of 'I', 'me' and 'my' throughout the poem. This is inevitable in a monologue – i.e. people will naturally refer to 'I', 'me' and 'my' when referring to aspects of their own life. In considering what this tells the reader about the Duke, students may argue that the Duke is self-centred and self-important. He is proud and views his thoughts, feelings and opinions as central.

Activity 5 This activity asks students to closely read the poem to locate 'clues' about the Duke's murderous actions.

For this activity, perhaps ask the students to work in pairs, close reading and annotating the text to indicate each example of a 'clue' that hints that the Duke had his first wife murdered. Encourage students to appreciate that each layer of truth adds to the drama as we, the reader, feel as though we are bearing witness to the indirect confessions of a murderer. The drama is further enhanced due to the foreboding realisation that he may do this again to his prospective new wife.

Activity 6 This activity focuses students' attention on the reasons behind the Duke's actions.

The Duke is evidently excusing and justifying his actions by apportioning blame and provocation to the Duchess's behaviour. Some examples will include:

- She would smile at a view of the sunset.
- She would smile at gifts presented to her – he cites a bough of cherries.
- She would smile when riding her white horse.

His obvious jealousy would be angered by her innocent words of thanks or happy expression.

You could discuss with students whether they think this behaviour warrants the Duke's contempt.

Activity 7 This activity is a creative task designed to help students understand the motivations of the characters in the poem.

Whichever task students select, ensure that they are able to support any comments they make with evidence from the poem.

Stretch yourself This activity aims to help students gain further insight into the Duke's character.

Students should use this activity to reveal the Duke's belief that the family name, and the family traditions, should be valued above and beyond all

else. The Duke always has his reputation at the forefront of his mind; this is more important to him than caring for, and respecting, his wife. You could encourage students to research nobility in the Victorian era: for instance, they could learn about how important it was to marry appropriately.

Language and imagery

Activity 8 This activity asks students to study an annotation of a stanza and to comment on what the language tells the reader about the Duke's character.

a Students should pick out that the Duke was highly contemptuous of the Duchess. This contempt is clear in his condescending tone, 'too easily impressed; she liked whate'er/She looked on'. He was impatient with her and frustrated that his 'favor at her breast' would meet with the same response as the flattery of 'some officious fool'. This indicates how he felt that he should have been centre of her world and the focus of her attention.

b The exclamation mark in this stanza highlights the Duke's incredulity at the Duchess's behaviour. He is outraged at her supposed naïvety and neglectful attitude to him. The Duke is not being very fair to the Duchess; his possessive and jealous nature has turned what should have been respect for her modesty and sweet nature, to disdain.

Activity 9 This activity draws the students' attention to the close of the poem.

Students might consider the fact that the work of art being referred to depicts the idea of one being 'tamed'. This is perhaps forewarning as to what the next Duchess might expect or how he would want her to be. The warning, on a sinister note, hints that if the next Duchess is not tamed to his will, then the same 'commands' (line 45) may be issued toward her.

Structure and form

Activity 10 This activity directs students' attention to the use of rhyming couplets in the poem.

Students should note how the joyful and pleasing rhyme and beat of the couplet contrasts with the sinister confession of a murderer. This is effective because the lyrical flow of words presented masks an ominous and disturbing truth.

Activity 11 This activity asks students to examine the use of enjambement in the poem.

The following annotated paragraph comments on the effect of some examples of enjambement:

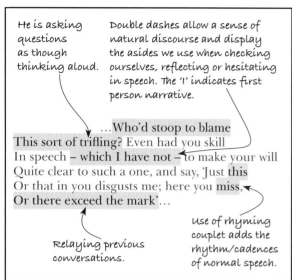

He is asking questions as though thinking aloud.

Double dashes allow a sense of natural discourse and display the asides we use when checking ourselves, reflecting or hesitating in speech. The 'I' indicates first person narrative.

...Who'd stoop to blame
This sort of trifling? Even had you skill
In speech – which I have not – to make your will
Quite clear to such a one, and say, 'Just this
Or that in you disgusts me; here you miss,
Or there exceed the mark'...

Relaying previous conversations.

Use of rhyming couplet adds the rhythm/cadences of normal speech.

Students are reminded that they looked at enjambement and its effects in Chapter 5.

Personal response

Activity 12 This activity requires a personal response from students.

Students are likely to feel that the Duchess has been treated unfairly and therefore will feel sympathy for her. You could encourage students to think about the Duchess's viewpoint by asking them to write a diary entry by her.

'The Ruined Maid' by Thomas Hardy

This poem is suitable for students entered for the Foundation Tier. It presents a conversation between two Victorian ladies, one of whom has had a dramatic change in social status.

Meaning

Activity 1 This activity asks students to think about the word 'ruined' before they read the poem.

Some students may be able to suggest accurate definitions. Direct them to the full title and ask them to consider why this term might be especially applicable to 'maids'.

Activity 2 This activity directs students to the contrasts between the two characters.

This activity allows the students to closely examine the poem in relation to detail around key points of character. If some students are unsure where to start, use the starting examples provided in the grid below:

	Amelia	Amelia's friend
Appearance	Fine garments, gay bracelets, bright feathers, fine sweeping gown, little gloves, healthy glow.	Clothes in tatters, no shoes or socks, described as 'raw'.
Attitude	Quite aloof, condescending to her friend.	Amazed at Amelia's transformation, showers her with praise.
Voice (dialect, tone etc.)	Minimal speech, formal language (until the final line), use of 'one', tone is proud and standoffish.	Colloquial speech, lots of enthusiastic speech to show her surprise, tone is incredulous.
Daily life	The reader gets the impression that Amelia does not have many duties as she is able to 'strut about Town' and keep her appearance immaculate.	Amelia's friend seems to have a hard life full of labour such as 'digging potatoes'. She is not able to wear fine clothes and live a life of leisure.

This activity is replaced on Worksheet 7d in the online resources.

Activity 3 This activity focuses students' attention on the use and effect of dialect in the poem.

a Students should notice that the dialect allows the reader to see the contrast between the statuses of the two women. A strong regional dialect indicates a lack of education and low social standing.

b Encourage students to initially identify each example of Dorset dialect in the poem. After working in pairs to attempt a translation, support student discussion around the effect the dialect brings to the poem. Students might consider a range of ideas from highlighting the contrast between the farm maid and the newly refined Amelia to providing a platform for Hardy's comments on the plight of individuals as a result of economic and class restrictions.

c This part of the activity requires a personal response from the students. Ask students to discuss, and clarify, their point of view. Both interpretations can be supported.

d Students might explore the idea that Hardy is intentionally highlighting the fact that Amelia may wear new clothes and have a little more money, but in essence she cannot escape her real self – and class. She may have escaped her lowly origins but she is unable to escape aspects of her birth and education of her class.

Students are reminded that they looked at accent and dialect earlier in the chapter.

Activity 4 This activity reminds students of the significance of the title.

Guide students who might find themselves struggling. Perhaps students will identify Hardy's critical comments on the plights of women in Victorian society and how society itself, owing to its exploitation of women, 'ruins' them and their prospects.

Stretch yourself This activity will require a creative and personal response from the students. This could be used as an assessed Speaking and listening exercise.

Language and imagery

Activity 5 This activity focuses on the sound of the dialect used in the poem.

a Students should use this first section to explore the Dorset dialect and the acquired London accent of Amelia – using this as a means to heighten the contrasts between them.

b This part of the activity encourages students to focus on Hardy's perspective. Some students may consider the fact that the tone, while apparently light hearted and quite comical, allows Hardy to make a critical comment on Victorian society and how it exploits women from a range of economic and class backgrounds – i.e. who is indeed the more ruined of the two? Many of Hardy's poems feature the plights, situations and dilemmas faced by women at this time, whether from the city streets or the rural countryside.

Structure and form

Activity 6 This activity looks at the structure and rhyme of the poem.

Take students carefully through the annotated extract in detail. Allow students to choose their own stanza in order to annotate and comment on how the comic tone contrasts with the serious point Hardy is making. If students struggle, you could present the following example:

> The image of Amelia's face being 'blue and bleak' with dirt and fatigue from the hard labour contrasts starkly with her now 'delicate cheek' as a lady of leisure.
>
> "Your hands were like paws then, your face blue and bleak
> But now I'm bewitched by your delicate cheek,
> And your little gloves fit as on any la-dy!"
> "We never do work when we're ruined," said she.
>
> This adds a comic lilt to the speech of Amelia's friend, which is emphasised by the exclamation mark.

Activity 7 This activity examines the reasons for Hardy giving his characters a voice.

a In order to respond to the first section of this activity, ask students to mind map all the advantages that we get from this dialogue that we don't get from the monologue found in 'My Last Duchess'. Students might comment on how:

- the dialogue allows the key character's actions to be questioned, hearing their responses. This allows the key characters to 'explain' some of their thoughts and decisions.
- more than one perspective on Victorian society and conditions is offered.

b This part of the activity supports student analysis of the fact that Hardy is giving these women a voice at a time when women would not have been given a voice to comment freely. Victorian society was very patriarchal and, as such, women were not given the freedom to comment on situations in the same way as they are today. Hardy, through his characterisation of these two women, allows them to critique a society that exploited women morally, socially and economically via unwritten social codes.

Activity 8 This activity looks at the final lines in the poem.

Allow students to survey and offer a range of responses. Some points of consideration might refer to a selection of the following:

- The title refers to Amelia, therefore it is only fitting that the last line comes from her.
- Hardy gives this 'ruined' woman a voice, up to the last line. He gives her a sense of purpose and importance in a society that is well versed in not listening to the words of women.
- To leave the reader with a tinge of sadness – we see Amelia reveal a sense of who she once was and still can't avoid being: her situation seems poignant and gloomy as we realise that she has condemned herself to life as an 'outsider'; her future is austere.

Activity 9 This activity asks students to discuss the refrain.

Take a range of responses, ensuring students validate their opinion. One approach is to look first at each refrain individually and then in turn; do they differ in meaning and delivery? Students should then explore the refrain as a whole, tracking how the word possibly changes from a tone of sarcasm and irony to one of sadness and pathos. The repetition also alludes to the repeated sentiment in Victorian society – how the 'moral code' is forever levelled at women. Students may also comment that the refrain, like the chorus in a song, has a musical quality which heightens the comic effect of the rhyme scheme.

Personal response

Activity 10 This activity requires a personal response from students.

This activity will need students to look at the layers of inference explored by Hardy. On the one hand, Hardy will be strongly aware that a woman's life will be 'ruined' by the judgmental Victorian society should she overstep the sexual moral code. However, alternatively, he perhaps offers some retaliation on society in this poem as Amelia 'appears' to be the one who has the better life of the two women. Nurture discussion around this topic and take a range of valid responses with exemplification from the text.

'Brendon Gallacher' by Jackie Kay

This poem is suitable for students entered for the Foundation Tier. It presents Kay's memories of her imaginary friend Brendon Gallacher from her childhood.

Meaning

Activity 1 This activity is a sequencing activity and will help students approach the content of the poem.

The correct order is: d, e, c, b, h, f, g, a.

Students are reminded that they looked at how to sequence poems in Chapter 4.

Activity 2 This activity asks students to focus their knowledge of Brendon Gallacher in a spider diagram.

Suggestions for what the readers discover about Brendon Gallacher are that:

- he is 7
- he is Irish
- his father is in prison as he was a cat burglar
- he has six brothers
- he is poor
- his mother drinks
- he has spiky hair, an impish grin and a funny, flapping ear.

Activity 3 This activity asks students to consider how and why Kay writes about Brendon Gallacher.

Some of this answer requires a personal response but students may suggest that they started to wonder if he was real when she would not bring him round to dinner as he had 'big holes in his trousers.' However, most students may state that they did not notice he was not real until her mother explains 'there are no Gallachers at 24 Novar./ There never have been any Gallachers next door.' The discovery is quite shocking but Kay does not reveal that he was not real as she wants her readers to see that Brendon Gallacher was an important friend, even though he was imaginary. If it were made explicit that Brendon Gallacher was imaginary, the reader may not take her feelings for him seriously.

Activity 4 This activity focuses students' attention on Kay's presentation of Glasgow.

Students may suggest that Kay uses her friend to project her own feelings about growing up in Glasgow. She wanted to go 'some place nice. Some place far' so it appears that she did not overly enjoy growing up in the city.

Activity 5 This activity asks students to think about Kay's motivation in composing this poem.

In writing 'Brendon Gallacher' when she is older, Kay may be stating that it is acceptable (and not unheard of) to have an imaginary friend when you are young. She does not believe that it is anything to be ashamed of.

Language and imagery

Activity 6 This activity directs students to Kay's use of repetition.

Students should select the first bullet.

Activity 7 This activity looks at Kay's dialect in the poem.

One suggestion would be 'wee' for small. It helps us to hear the poet's voice telling the story, which makes it more authentic and personal.

Activity 8 This activity asks students to examine Kay's use of speech.

This answer requires a personal response and it might be too simplistic merely to choose one of the options. One interpretation is that Kay has included speech as it affected her a great deal. She will still remember what her mother said to her. It therefore makes the situation appear more real. You would lose the impact of discovering that he is not real if it was delivered as part of the narrative. It is more dramatic for the mother to reveal that she knows he does not live at '24 Novar.'

Structure and form

Activity 9 This activity focuses students' attention on word placement in the poem.

Kay wanted to emphasise how important Brendon Gallacher was to her. Also, the lines often end with an 'er' sound which gives the poem a song-like rhythm.

Activity 10 This activity looks at line length in the poem.

The lines are shorter in the final stanza as it is matter of fact. He dies and we get a brief description of him. The punctuation slows the rhythm of the poem down as she laments his loss.

Personal response

Activity 11 This activity mostly requires a personal response but her dislike of Glasgow and her small family have been mentioned in previous answers. Ask the class if she necessarily needed to have an unhappy childhood to create Brendon Gallacher; could she also invent Brendon Gallacher if she was happy? Would he have been different?

Stretch yourself This activity is intended to inspire students to think creatively and to explore a different literary genre – the short story. This activity should highlight the opportunities and limitations of both forms.

Students are reminded that they looked at changing prose into verse in Chapter 5.

'On a Portrait of a Deaf Man' by John Betjeman

Interactive activity: John Betjeman's 'On a Portrait of a Deaf Man'

This poem is suitable for students entered for both Foundation and Higher Tiers. It presents Betjeman reminiscing about his father.

Meaning

Activity 1 This activity is intended to help students familiarise themselves with the concept of a portrait.

a This requires a personal response from the students. Encourage them to be as detailed and honest as they can.

b This builds on the first section. Some students may find it easy/hard to sum up their chosen person into just six parts. Hold class discussion on this: who found it easy/who found it hard? Was there any reason for this?

Activity 2 This activity focuses on the detail learned about Betjeman's father.

This activity encourages students to track and close read the poem. Should students need further teacher modelling, use the following two extra examples:

Quote from poem	What we learn
'The kind old face'	Betjeman's father was kind.
'he liked … potatoes in their skin'	His father liked to eat jacket potatoes.
'… and painted it in oil'	He was creative and liked to paint.

This activity is replicated on Worksheet 7e in the online resources.

Activity 3 This activity focuses students' attention on how Betjeman refers to his father.

For this activity, start by asking students to highlight all the references Betjeman makes when referring to his father. A starting point for some students might be that Betjeman never refers to his father as such, as he is emotionally distancing himself from the pain his father's death/from the loss of his father. The memory of his father's death still hurts and he is still unable to embrace this fully or directly.

Stretch yourself This activity demands a personal response from the students. Encourage textual exemplification to support their views. One view may be: when someone dies, many people question God why that person has had to die/be taken from us. Betjeman is perhaps questioning his faith here. The fact that he is still addressing 'God' implies he still, to whatever extent, acknowledges a 'God' and the desire to believe his father's soul will still live on. However, the more practical side of Betjeman questions this as he 'only sees decay'.

Language and imagery

Activity 4 This activity will require the students to choose another stanza and annotate it following the model given.

a Their annotations should highlight what effect such morbid imagery is intended to have on the reader. An example could be:

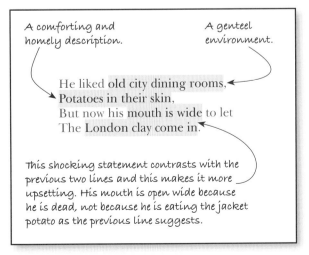

A comforting and homely description.

A genteel environment.

He liked old city dining rooms,
Potatoes in their skin,
But now his mouth is wide to let
The London clay come in.

This shocking statement contrasts with the previous two lines and this makes it more upsetting. His mouth is open wide because he is dead, not because he is eating the jacket potato as the previous line suggests.

Students are reminded that they looked at the effect of contrast in Chapter 4.

b When commenting on the effect of this morbid imagery, students should make reference to the shocking contrasts that Betjeman introduces; we are lulled into an image of domestic comforts and then sharply reminded that the father is dead. This makes the first half of the stanzas more poignant.

Activity 5 This activity will require a personal response from the students. However, you may wish to use the following as a springboard into this activity:

● his father – proud, respectful, full of admiration

● religion – sceptical, dubious, angry

● the prospect of death – fearful, apprehensive.

Structure and form

Activity 6 This activity asks students to examine the rhyme-scheme.

a Students may comment that it symbolises the steady, predictable and reassuring presence of his father in his life. It signifies the stability his father offered and gave him.

b The rhyme pattern of each stanza is abcb. The lines that rhyme heavily contrast in terms of content, the second line describing a fond memory and the fourth line containing a morbid image.

Activity 7 This activity asks students to consider the tone of the final line.

This will evoke different responses in students. Ask students to justify their responses, drawing their focus back to the poem as a whole and the overall impression they get from it. Further encourage some students to read the last line aloud in the tone they are suggesting.

Personal response

Activity 8 This activity requires a personal response from students.

Students should offer explanation and exemplification when offering their point of view. Students are likely to feel that Betjeman's father was a kind and loving man and that their relationship was strong. This can be deduced from the positive details Betjeman offers the reader about his father.

Comparing poems in the 'Characters and voices' cluster

🔊 Analysis activity: Comparing 'The Clown Punk' and 'Ozymandias'

🔊 Analysis activity: Comparing 'My Last Duchess' and 'The Ruined Maid'

🔊 Viewpoints activity: Comparing 'The River God' and 'My Last Duchess'

🔊 Planning activity: Comparing poems from 'Characters and voices'

🔊 Planning activity: Comparing two poems of your choice from the cluster.

At the end of this chapter, students are provided with some guidance as to how to approach the comparison element of the Anthology examination question (Unit 2A). In the exam, students will be asked to analyse a set poem from the 'Characters and voices' cluster; this could be any poem from the cluster so it is important that students are prepared to respond confidently to all of the poems in this cluster. Students will also be asked to analyse one other poem of their choice from the cluster in light of the focus of the question. For example, students may be asked:

> Compare how voice is presented in 'My Last Duchess' and one other poem from the 'Characters and voices' cluster.

Analysing the question

It is of vital importance that students understand what is being asked of them in the exam. A sample question is annotated in the Student Book with the five key elements that students are required to address:

1 A **comparison** must be made

2 The poet's **techniques** must be examined

3 The **focus area** must be clear in students' minds

4 The **named poem** must be covered in the student's response

5 One **other** poem must be included in the analysis.

Activity 1 This activity asks students to annotate further sample questions in the same way to consolidate their learning.

Choosing your comparison poem

Remind students that the choice they make regarding the second poem they are to analyse is crucial. They need to select a poem that will provide them with enough material to enable them to make a full and effective comparison – both in terms of the similarities between the poems and also the differences between them. Students should be able to compare:

- the attitudes and ideas presented
- the language and imagery used
- the structure and form of the poems.

Students have been working through the poems presented in this chapter according to these areas of analysis. The chapters of Section A, where these different aspects are individually introduced and explored, will provide further assurance for students wishing to revise the sort of techniques and devices they should be looking out for.

In planning their response, students are encouraged to record their initial ideas in a grid. This will help to direct their thoughts and discourage them from straying from the focus of the question. It will also enable them to see the similarities and differences between the two poems. The grid provided uses 'Brendon Gallacher' as an example.

Activity 2 This activity asks students to complete their own grid using an alternative comparison poem of their choice. This should illustrate to students that a variety of poems can be chosen for comparison – but that some choices are more effective than others.

This activity is replicated on Worksheet 7f in the online resources.

Structuring your answer

Once students are clear about what they need to do, and the points they wish to cover, they can think about their opening paragraph. Encourage students to use this paragraph both for their own reference (to outline what they intend to cover in their essay) and to ensure that they are clearly establishing the focus of their response for the examiner. This paragraph should immediately demonstrate skills of comparison. A sample paragraph is provided.

Activity 3 This activity asks students to write their own opening paragraph for their chosen comparison.

Students are then advised to draw on discourse markers to illustrate points of comparison in the main section of their response.

It is worth reinforcing at this stage that students should remember to consider the differences and contrasts between poems in addition to examining the similarities between them.

Activity 4 This activity asks students to write a paragraph in which they develop their comparison with the poem of their choice and underline the words that indicate that a comparison is being made. This should reinforce with students the need to constantly compare one poem with another.

Reinforce with students the need to explain **how** and **why** a poet is creating certain effects rather than simply recounting which devices a poet has used. Also encourage students to make a personal response; examiners will be looking for evidence of engagement with the text.

Students are finally advised to make an insightful comment in their closing paragraph to illustrate that they are comparing the poems to the end of their essay.

Activity 5 This activity asks students to write their final paragraph and to include their final pertinent point.

Students could contribute alternative questions to help them to become comfortable with the structure of the question. This would encourage them to think about potential pairings of poems in readiness for the exam.

Remind students to bear in mind the theme of 'Characters and voices' throughout their analysis. What do the poems they are writing about offer in an exploration of this theme?

Outcomes

In this chapter students have learned how to:

- approach analysing poems in the 'Characters and voices' cluster
- compare two poems in the cluster.

AO focus

AO1: Respond to texts critically and imaginatively; select and evaluate relevant textual detail to illustrate and support interpretation.

AO2: Explain how language, structure and form contribute to writers' presentation of ideas, themes and settings.

AO3: Make comparisons and explain links between texts, evaluating writers' different ways of expressing meaning and achieving effects.

In this chapter your students will:

- explore the theme of place in poetry
- analyse and comment on the meaning, language, imagery, structure and form of a selection of poems from the 'Place' cluster of their Anthology through close reading and investigation activities
- explain poems in relation to social, cultural and historical settings
- strengthen their own understanding and use of poetic terms
- gain confidence in making a personal response to the poems they read.

In this chapter, students analyse a sample selection of the poems from the 'Place' cluster of the Anthology. The key aspects of analysis that students covered in Section A of the Student Book: meaning (Chapter 1), language (Chapter 2), imagery (Chapter 3), structure (Chapter 4) and verse form (Chapter 5), now shape the progression of activities in Section B, so that for each poem in turn, students are asked to answer questions on meaning, language and imagery, structure and form and personal response. The addition of personal response here reflects the need for students to engage with texts on an individual level – something examiners will be looking for evidence of. It is hoped that this consistent and logical approach will help to demystify the study of poetry and increase students' confidence by equipping them with a clear method with which to apply their skills of analysis.

Key terms

Key terms the students are introduced to in this chapter:

- Persona
- Oxymoron
- Modifier
- Present tense
- Personification
- Protagonist

Poems included in this chapter

Six of the poems from this cluster are covered in the Student Book, the remainder are covered in the online resources. The poems covered in the Student Book are written by a range of male and female poets, both contemporary and from the Literary Heritage. All of the poems in this chapter are suitable for students studying both Foundation and Higher Tiers, with the exception of 'Spellbound' which is suitable for Foundation Tier students.

Poems covered in this chapter:

- 'Cold Knap Lake' by Gillian Clarke
- 'The Wild Swans at Coole' by W B Yeats
- 'London' by William Blake
- 'Spellbound' by Emily Brontë
- 'Wind' by Ted Hughes
- 'Neighbours' by Gillian Clarke

Poems from the 'Place' cluster covered by online resources:

- Interactive activity: Vocabulary in 'Below the Green Corrie'
- Interactive activity: Responding to 'A Vision' by Simon Armitage
- Viewpoints activity: Understanding 'The Moment' by Margaret Atwood
- Analysis activity: A close look at the 'The Blackbird of Glanmore'
- Interactive activity: 'Price We Pay for the Sun' by Grace Nichols
- Interactive activity: Responding to 'Hard Water' by Jean Sprackland
- Analysis activity: A close look at 'The Prelude'
- Analysis activity: Analysing 'Storm in the Black Forest' by D H Lawrence

Additional resources

Worksheets:

- 8a: Introductory activity
- 8b: 'The Wild Swans at Coole' Activity 1
- 8c: 'London' Activity 1
- 8d: 'Wind' Activity 1

- 8e: 'Wind' Activity 2b
- Choosing your comparison poem

Audio recordings of some of the poems used in this chapter are also available in the online resources, including some alternative readings.

Getting started

The theme of place is introduced here to encourage students to think about why this is an area that poets choose to write about. They are invited to think about the different emotional responses that places can evoke. The poems that are covered in this chapter explore a range of places and the effect that they have on the voice of the poem. Some of the places presented reinforce how we can be comforted by a place and emphasise their uplifting and soothing effect, whereas some of the poems convey the threat that some places pose, and emphasise the fear and loneliness that they can evoke. At the beginning of the activities for each poem, the theme of place is reinforced and students are encouraged to think about why each particular poem appears in this cluster and what it has to offer in an exploration of this theme.

Throughout the chapter, students are reminded that they should always consider the theme of this cluster and think about what the individual poets are saying about place in each of the poems. The activities, therefore, continually link back to this theme while exploring different aspects of analysis.

Activity This introductory activity is designed to get students to consider how different settings can nurture a range of responses and emotions: positive and negative. The activity will be very personal to the individual, but in turn will highlight how some places have the same effect on others. Encourage students to enhance their responses with descriptive detail and to explore fully the emotional response they had to their chosen place. Some students may be willing to share their place and attached emotions with the class. Do any students have any places in common? Are their reasons similar/different?

An alternative starter activity to help students explore the theme of place could be to think of an event/incident that they can remember. It can be something that happened to them or something that they saw happen to someone else. Ask students to write down the event/incident in a circle in the middle of a sheet of paper. They should create a spider diagram of what they can remember, under the following headings, and in as much detail as possible. Stress that they do not need to write in full sentences.

- Summary of event
- Who was present?
- What sensory details can they recall: smell, sound, touch, taste, sight?
- Where did the incident take place?
- Why do they think this incident happened?
- When did the incident take place: year, month, time of day, etc?
- What feelings do they associate with this incident?

Students should then share and discuss their recollections with a partner.

This activity is replicated on Worksheet 8a in the online resources.

Working through the chapter

Background information is given for each of the six poems in this chapter. Some biographical information is given about each poet and some introductory information about each poem is provided so that students can contextualise poems before embarking on a full analysis.

Of course, you may not have time in the classroom to explore each of the poems in the cluster in as much detail as is explored in the Student Book. The material that is presented here is intended as a suggested 'ideal' model of approach but you may only be able to select certain areas to focus on. It is hoped that you will be able to apply some, if not all, of this approach – however, it is by no means prescriptive and should not be interpreted as the number of activities that students will 'need' to have completed in preparation for their exam.

The personal response activities are crucial but by their nature are problematic to assess. For these activities, some guidance regarding the sort of response students are likely to submit is given, but this by no means should be taken as 'correct'. Students should be encouraged to engage with the poems on a personal level and to feel confident in voicing their interpretations as long as they can be supported by evidence from the poem text.

Before the poems are looked at in detail, students could be reminded of the guidance on how to read a poem, guidance they met in the Section A introduction. This summarises all the key areas that they should pay attention to as they read the Anthology poems for the first time.

'Cold Knap Lake' by Gillian Clarke

This poem is suitable for students entered for both Foundation and Higher Tiers. It presents the poet exploring her memory of a place which has had a lasting effect on her.

Meaning

Activity 1 This activity is intended to help students get to grips with the content of the poem.

Students could adopt the 'who, what, where, why and how' (the five Ws) approach to their first level of analysis of the poem when creating their spider diagram. As a consolidating exercise, put the headings on the board and ask students to come out and log their responses. Ensure, as a class, you are in full agreement about the key five Ws.

Activity 2 This activity asks the students to undertake a task of close reading and interpretation.

Some examples of remembered facts might include:

- Her mum was wearing a cotton frock/'her wartime cotton frock'.
- The dying girl had cold blue lips/'blue-lipped and ...'
- The onlookers were entranced and watched silently/'the crowd stood silent'.

Ensure the students validate their point with actual quotation.

Language and imagery

Activities 3 and 4 These activities ask students to consider Clarke's use of colour.

To help students answer this question, perhaps project the same colours (including hues of colours) onto the whiteboard. This should highlight the contrast of the cold and deathly blue colour against the warmth and reassuring rosy-red colour crafted in the poem. Allow students to offer such suggestions as life/death, cold/warmth and loss/love and discuss how this affects their interpretation of the tone of the poem. It is not accidental that Clarke showers her mother in colours of warmth and love – not only as a result of her heroic act but also as characteristic of her personality.

When they are writing their own paragraph, encourage students to refer to quotations from the poem and to think about how the use of colour has affected their 'vision' of the scene Clarke describes.

Activity 5 This activity focuses students' attention on the language used in the fourth stanza.

a When annotating the remainder of the stanza, ensure your students are picking up on:

- the imagery of the mud
- the alliteration in 'webs', 'swan' and 'wings'
- the internal rhyme in 'treading', 'heavy' and 'webs'
- the onomatopoeic language 'beat' and 'whistle'.

b The impression of the lake created here is that it is an ominous place of potential danger and cold isolation.

Structure and form

Activity 6 This activity asks students to comment on the structure of the poem.

It has a loose but fairly clear structure, with stanzas of four and six lines being repeated. The poem ends in a rhyming couplet. Clarke demonstrates that there is a thread of certainty to strains of a memory. However, Clarke also highlights that often there is an element of uncertainty to aspects of this 'recollected' memory, which she further alludes to through the looseness in the structure, i.e. can we be totally sure what lies beneath the surface of our supposed memories? Ensure that students are confident with the new stanza terminology here before moving on.

Activity 7 This activity encourages the students to decipher a statement of Clarke's: 'Was I there?'

Take valid and appropriate answers from the students encouraging them to justify this with reference to the text. One suggestion might be that Clarke is commenting on how memories can become 'changed' over time, how they can become extensions of things heard, not necessarily witnessed. Was Clarke actually there, or does the 'memory' feel like a memory because she has heard it, and visualised it, after it was told to her by others?

Activity 8 This activity requires students to examine Clarke's closing metaphor, 'all lost things lie under closing water'.

Clarke uses the place and this childhood memory to contemplate 'memories' altogether. This first line, of the closing rhyming couplet, sees Clarke consider how some memories can lie just beneath the surface of recollection and how, although appeared lost, can be called to mind and revived – just like that of the life of the little drowning girl.

Stretch yourself This activity is aimed at those students who have grasped the dual nature of this poem. You may like to start their thinking by drawing a table of two columns which students can complete in pairs. This could be an opportunity to explore contrast and its effect in a broader sense. Students are introduced to the technique of contrast in Chapter 4.

Personal response

Activity 9 This activity asks students to analyse the poem by examining why it is suggestive of a fairytale.

Ask the students to brainstorm what elements of a typical fairytale we find in this poem. Some suggestions might include: a dramatic rescue, a heroine and a poor family. Students may make the link between a childhood memory and the recollection of fairytales, short stories and nursery rhymes being read to us as children. Can childhood memories merge with childhood stories told? Do our childhood memories become accentuated with hints of fairytale/dreamlike drama?

'The Wild Swans at Coole' by W B Yeats

This poem is suitable for students entered for both Foundation and Higher Tiers. It presents the poet visiting a place which causes him to reflect upon his life.

Meaning

Activity 1 This activity takes students into the heart of the seasonal setting of the poem.

Share students' findings, not only from their own expectations but also from what they find in Yeats's poem. Examples from Yeats's poem include dry woodland paths and the brimming water levels in the lake.

You could instigate a general discussion about which emotions students typically associate with autumn. Does the season have certain emotional links for them and why?

This activity is replicated on Worksheet 8b in the online resources.

Activity 2 This activity asks students to consider the poet's feelings.

This activity requires a personal response from the students, building on the examples already provided in the Student Book. Remind students here of the biographical background of Yeats's visits.

Activity 3 This activity asks students to focus on Yeats's use of the swans to express his own feelings.

a A suggested analysis might be: to Yeats, the swans never age; they always look the same and appear to take part in the same activities. For Yeats, his life has changed over the 19 years, so he feels the opposite and they become,

therefore, a tool for contrast. The swans remind him of his former freshness and youth – something he feels he has lost and will never have again.

b The second part to this activity alludes to one swan not having a 'pairing'. He sees himself in that swan, alone perhaps, and dejected.

c The final section of this activity asks students to focus on the modifier 'wild' that is found in the title. This is a graphic image and alludes to the fact that the swans are not domesticated. Yeats illustrates that the swans do not nest at Coole and are therefore free to fly to another place. This freedom is something Yeats appears to envy – the power of freedom and lack of restraint.

Language and imagery

Activity 4 This activity asks students to create their own simile based on the autumnal imagery in the poem.

Encourage students to be imaginative and to use vivid, descriptive language in their similes. As students share their responses, ask how each simile makes them feel. Write some of the examples given on the board as a backdrop to the lesson.

Activity 5 This activity allows a deeper level of exploration from the students, focusing their analytical eye on three specific areas of language.

Some suggestions might include:

- **Colour**: 'autumn' – gold, red, oranges of the flora; 'October twilight' – soft, golden twinkling of the stars; 'swans' – brilliant and dazzling white feathers.

- **Sound**: 'paths are dry' – cracking and creaking of twigs underfoot; 'clamorous wings' – swift and sharp beat of birds' wings; 'paddle in the cold' – splash and splatter of water.

- **Movement**: 'still sky' – a quiet stillness; 'all suddenly mount' – the initial commencement of the swans' flight; 'they paddle' – quirky, bathing and swimming of the swans.

Structure and form

Activity 6 This activity asks students to look at Yeats's use of repetition.

a 'Still' is repeated four times. A suggested reading of this repetition may refer to the stillness of nature; while man changes, grows old and weary, nature appears not to change. Does nature age as man does? This reflects Yeats's contemplative and sombre mood.

b Ensure that the examples of repetition selected are valid and that students have explored how this affects the reader's interpretation. Some valid responses include: wings, twilight and water.

Activity 7 This activity introduces students to the shifts in time in the poem.

Some examples include:

- Past: 'I have looked upon those brilliant creatures'.
- Present: 'The trees are in their autumn beauty'.
- Future: 'Among what rushes will they build'.

Yeats is thinking about the different stages of his life because Coole allows him to 'clear his head' and think freshly about the progression of his life.

Students are reminded that they looked at changes in time in Wilfred Owen's poem 'Disabled' in Chapter 4.

Activity 8 This activity requires the students to examine the phrase, 'all's changed ...'

By now students will be aware of Yeats's reflective and melancholy mood as the backdrop to this poem. Encourage them to make the extension of understanding to note that this 'change' relates to his life/lost youth/lost love. The major change appears to be within himself. In his younger days, when he first witnessed the swans at Coole, he 'trod with a lighter tread'; he was 'unwearied'. As he watches on this occasion, he is powerfully aware of the changes. Coole gives him a sense of perspective that he does not gain from other places.

Personal response

Activity 9 This activity again asks students to consider how Yeats feels after conducting a more thorough analysis of the poem.

You could open this up into a class discussion of the poem's tone.

Activity 10 This activity encourages students to contemplate the statements 'in my twilight years' and 'in the autumn of life' in relation to this poem.

Ask students to discuss what these statements might mean. Have they heard them used before? Students should try to focus on the fact that for Yeats, the season of autumn reminds him of his stage of life, i.e. no longer in his youth and aware of his own mortality. Draw students' attention to the fact that 'autumn' and 'twilight' are both repeated in this poem, with Yeats clearly emphasising his sadness – as well as possibly fear – about the future.

Stretch yourself This activity should be used to explore the theme of lost love (with particular reference to Maud Gonne to whom he proposed several times). Suggested responses might include:

- 'broken rings' – alludes to marriage bands
- 'lover by lover'

- 'bell – beat' – church bells?
- 'nine and fifty swans' – one swan is clearly not 'paired' and therefore alone.

You could here remind students of the importance of contextual information when analysing poetry and how it can enhance their analysis and appreciation.

'London' by William Blake

This poem is suitable for students entered for both Foundation and Higher Tiers. It sees Blake making a comment about society through a disparaging depiction of the city of London. In order to understand the historical context of a poem, some of the more unfamiliar language is explored before the activities.

Meaning

Activity 1 This activity requires students to trace and log all that the persona of the poem sees and hears as he walks through the streets of London at midnight in a bid to strengthen students' appreciation of the sensory detail portrayed by Blake. Students could note the following.

What is seen	Evidence from the poem	What is heard	Evidence from the poem
A London street	'each chartered street'	Men's cries	'cry of every man'
The River Thames	'near where the chartered Thames does flow'	Baby's cries	'infant's cry of fear'
People's faces	'every face I meet'	Young women giving birth	'youthful harlot's curse'
Misery	'marks of woe'		

This activity is replicated on Worksheet 8c in the online resources.

Activity 2 This activity asks students to consider Blake's motivation in composing this poem.

Students should build on the information supplied in the Student Book. Blake was deeply critical and saddened by charters that allocated ownership and rights to certain individuals. Blake believed that such charters were robbing the ordinary people of London of their freedoms and rights. He is being heavily ironic in suggesting that even the river is not free. Students may find it beneficial to carry out some basic research about Blake and his views to answer this question. Extend the debate with the students to discuss Blake's views on man's destructive force over nature.

Language and imagery

Activity 3 This activity asks students to consider a metaphor in the poem.

Before you guide students to examine the powerful metaphor, 'mind-forged manacles,' ensure they are comfortable with the poetic term 'metaphor'. Next, ask students to consider where manacles might be used. Extend the discussion to try to get students to interpret what comment Blake is trying to make through the use of this metaphor. One suggested answer might be: building on the knowledge that manacles are like handcuffs, he is implying that people's thoughts and minds are too often limited, controlled and restricted in some way. He is frustrated and angered by this; by the robbing of people's free thought and ability to think independently.

Activity 4 This activity focuses students' attention on Blake's use of language.

Allow students the opportunity to log as many words as they can. Share the students' findings, ensuring that they have covered each of them. Students will highlight a range of feelings that Blake has about London society at this time, ranging from angry and saddened, to frustrated and despairing. Some examples of words with a negative effect include:

- 'weakness'
- 'woe'
- 'cry'
- 'blackening'
- 'sigh'
- 'blood'
- 'blights'
- 'plagues'.

Activity 5 This activity asks students to make a comment about an annotated part of the poem and in doing so, allows them to practise forming full written responses.

a It may prove beneficial to provide some further context of the social, historical and economic climate at the time with respect to this activity. Encourage students to spend some time researching the French Revolution. (In 1789, the French people revolted against the monarchy and aristocracy. This revolution was particularly bloody and violent.) It is this revolution that Blake alludes to as well as giving the warning that, if things do not change, then similar acts may follow in England. An effective paragraph should refer to Blake's use of alliteration, shocking imagery, vivid use of colour and stinging satire.

b This activity requires a personal response from the students. Students should be prepared to justify their responses rather than making a general link. You might want to share/read out examples from students.

Activity 6 This activity asks students to consider social factors in Blake's time.

Students should use this activity to explore the opposing images of 'blackening' and 'appals' using the annotations provided. There is both a criticism of the church here, its inactivity in failing to aid the need of others (chimney sweeps were often very young children and the job itself was dangerous on many levels) and a fear of society's abandonment of religion.

Structure and form

Activity 7 This activity asks students to think about the rhythm of the poem.

The use of clear repetition and regular rhyme adds a simple nursery rhyme quality to the poem, which contrasts starkly with the gruesome imagery and serious message which is far from innocent. At this point, students who are enjoying Blake's poetry could be directed to some of his other work from the *Songs of Innocence* and *Songs of Experience* collection in which he often uses simple rhyme to convey serious issues.

Activity 8 This activity introduces students to a key oxymoron in the poem.

Again, this activity requires some understanding of the social, political and economic climate of the time in which Blake was writing. Research will uncover that the final stanza alludes to the sexually transmitted diseases that were spreading through society at this time. This oxymoron contrasts love and desire (marriage) with death and destruction (hearse) – the husband passing on/carrying such diseases after his liaison with the 'youthful harlot'. Encourage students to contemplate Blake's final sombre message/warning.

Personal response

Activity 9 This activity requires a personal response by the students.

The task will aid their analysis, and understanding, of the description crafted by Blake in the poem. Share examples of the students' work. Ask students why they chose certain adjectives and to comment on their effectiveness.

Ask students if the impression created by Blake differs from their own impression of London today.

Stretch yourself This activity allows students to focus on the tone and mood, while exploring the diction and imagery employed. Share examples of students' reworking of the poem. If a pairing is finding this activity particularly challenging:

- put two pairings of students together, to support each other
- choose extracts from the rewriting of one student pairing and read it out to the class, acting as a model of good practice.

Students are reminded that they looked at changing words to have a different effect on meaning in Chapter 2.

'Spellbound' by Emily Brontë

This poem is suitable for students entered for the Foundation Tier. It depicts a sense of awe and wonder at the force and power of nature.

Meaning

Activity 1 This activity asks students to consider the poem's title before reading the poem.

This activity requires a personal response from students. Consideration of what 'spellbound' means to students should be a good starting point. In what context might students expect to hear this term? Encourage students to justify their responses with reasoning and explanation. You could divide the class and allocate several words to each group, asking them to choose the most appropriate and to defend their response.

Activity 2 This activity is intended to help students to familiarise themselves with the content of the poem.

You could ask students to share their spider diagrams once complete. Try to manage the pairing process to ensure students benefit from the peer collaboration and support.

Language and imagery

Activity 3 This activity promotes analysis of the rhythm of 'Spellbound'.

To answer this question, students should consider how the power and force of nature can sometimes be unrelenting and pulsating. Does this definite rhythm and tempo mirror this force at all? To explore the rhythm of this poem, do a whole class reading aloud, stressing and emphasising words that emphasise the cadence and beat. Brontë is carried along by the force of her surroundings in much the same way as we, as readers, are carried along by the poem's rhythm.

Activity 4 This activity further allows students to appreciate how poets carefully craft and manipulate their art through the precise and particular selection of vocabulary.

Take individual responses from students, promoting exemplification and explanation. Some possible suggestions might include:

- *coldly* blow – sense of icy wind, chilling the persona to the core
- *tyrant* spell – personified, ominous foreboding, threatening atmosphere
- *bare* boughs – barren, bleak and austere landscape.

Activity 5 This activity explores the function of tense within the poem.

Evidence that this poem is written in the present tense includes: 'the night is ...', 'coldly blow', 'trees are bending ...' etc. When considering the effect of using present, as opposed to past, tense students should bear in mind how placing the persona in the present tense heightens the power of nature, increasing its hold on the paralysed persona. The past tense would dilute the impact and supremacy of nature.

Activity 6 This activity asks students to examine Brontë's use of alliteration and assonance.

You may need to consolidate students' understanding of assonance and alliteration as a starting point. Students are reminded that they learned about alliteration and assonance in Chapter 2.

The sound effects generated here enforce the natural landscape around her. For example, the repetition of 'b' is quite harsh and indicates the sparseness of the branches. The repetition of 'w' is soft and indicates the delicacy of the falling snow.

Possible responses might include:

- alliteration: 'bare boughs' and 'wild winds'
- assonance: 'night/tyrant'

Ensure that students examine the effect of these techniques.

Structure and form

Activity 7 This activity asks students to examine the structure of the poem.

The simplicity of the structure reflects the grand simplicity of the force of nature. It is a basic and eternal force and does not need to be represented in an overly detailed and gratuitous fashion. Brontë is in awe of its simple and uncomplicated power; adding too much embellishment would detract from its impressive might.

Activity 8 This activity draws students' attention to the last lines of each stanza.

The change from 'cannot' to 'will not' go indicates how Brontë has willingly succumbed to the force of nature by the end of the poem; she has undertaken a journey and now wishes to stay to take in its wonder.

Activity 9 This activity directs students to the poem's final line.

The final point, in combining the previous two, is the most accurate. Brontë is both fixed in place by the force of the wind and also by her sense of awe and exhilaration.

Activity 10 This activity is intended to draw students' attention to the narrative voice in the poem.

'I' and 'me' assert the identity of the voice in the face of such overwhelming force and reinforce the personal connection that is being made here; the surroundings are having a strong and profound effect.

Personal response

Activity 11 This activity is intended to focus students' thinking on the tone of the poem by inviting discussion of the term 'melancholy'.

Ensure that all students fully understand this term and encourage a class debate about whether this can be applied to the poem, referring continually back to the poem for textual support.

Activity 12 This activity asks students to think of a place that has inspired awe in them.

Ask students to fully explain why they felt this way and highlight any similarities with 'Spellbound'.

'Wind' by Ted Hughes

This poem is suitable for students entered for both Foundation and Higher Tiers. It presents the effect of a ferocious storm.

Meaning

Activity 1 This activity requires a personal response from the students as they explore the sensory detail of a wind storm.

Students will have to draw on their imagination in part, endeavouring to allot precise modifiers to best capture the detail of what they are describing. You could collate students' responses and create a display to form the backdrop of your class discussion of 'Wind'.

This activity is replicated on Worksheet 8d in the online resources.

Activity 2 This activity helps students examine the time frame to this poem and in turn the changing characteristics of the wind storm on both man and landscape.

Students should try to focus on times of the day including, 'night' (line 1), 'till day rose' (line 2) (dawn) and also 'noon' (line 9). One example has been provided in the Student Book and students should use this as a model.

This activity is replicated on Worksheet 8e in the online resources.

Language and imagery

Activity 3 This activity requires the students to inspect the examples of personification found in stanza one.

a Any of the bulleted points is valid if supported with evidence from the text. Possible responses might cover the point that the wind seems all encompassing, powerful and unrelenting. The active verbs, 'crashing', 'booming', 'stampeding', etc. intensify this energy and might of the wind as it takes control of its landscape. The personified wind seems to dominate and command.

b Students are requested to annotate more of this poem, identifying further examples of personification and commenting on them. Take valid and appropriate responses from the students.

Activity 4 This activity motivates the students to examine examples of onomatopoeia within the poem.

a Reading this poem aloud will aid this analysis. Perhaps project a copy of the poem on to your whiteboard and then ask students to come to the front of the class to highlight all examples found. Take valid responses. Some examples of alliteration/assonance that are onomatopoeic include: 'b̲a̲ng' and 'fl̲a̲p' (line 14) which highlight assonance and onomatopoeia.

b Through this we are drawn to the loud and threatening sounds of the power of the wind storm and its impact on the landscape.

Students are reminded that they looked at onomatopoeia in Chapter 2.

Activity 5 This activity requires students to locate and comment on the similes present in this poem.

Hughes's imagery serves to strengthen the detail which captures the almost unimaginable power of nature at work on this night. Similes to note include:

- 'like the lens of a mad eye' (line 8)
- 'like an iron bar' (line 16)
- 'like some fine green goblet' (line 17).

Students should take each simile and comment on the purpose and strength of each in turn and then as a whole.

Structure and form

Activity 6 This activity asks students to think about the poem's structure.

The first bullet is the most accurate.

Activity 7 This activity looks at enjambement and the effect this has on the poem's impression.

Hughes frequently captures the driving and powerful force of the wind. Examples of enjambement could likewise be said to be a driving force throughout the poem. Allow students to focus on specific examples and explore what is added by it.

Students are reminded that they looked at enjambement and its effect in Chapter 5.

Stretch yourself This activity asks students to explore the relationship between man and nature. Higher ability students should be able to comment on man's futility compared to the might of nature – that we should be humbled by it and respect its force as we have no power to stop it.

Personal response

Activity 8 This activity asks students to make a personal response to the poem.

When explaining their response to a partner, ensure that students are drawing on quotations from the text to back up their points.

'Neighbours' by Gillian Clarke

This poem is suitable for students entered for both Foundation and Higher Tiers. It describes the aftermath of the Chernobyl disaster and the effect on the surrounding countries.

Meaning

Activity 1 This activity requires a personal response from the students as they work together in a small group to explore the concept and meaning of the word 'neighbour'.

Do they feel the meaning has changed over time? Do they feel it means different things to different people, communities and cultures?

Activity 2 This activity asks students to consider the time of year in which this poem is set.

Context and setting are important aspects of poems and Clarke, setting this poem in the season of spring, ensures her reference is full of meaning and significance. Take valid responses from the students as they explore what they believe 'spring' could represent. Possible suggestions may state that spring should herald birth, rebirth, hope and regeneration: the cycle of life beginning with the budding of flowers and the birth of lambs. Clarke is making a human and political comment by emphasising the disturbance of natural and seasonal order as a direct result of this disaster – she uses images of death and destruction to highlight this.

Language and imagery

Activity 3 This activity requires students to examine the vivid imagery prevalent in this poem.

When exploring shocking and disturbing images such as, 'Crows drank from the lamb's eye' and 'each lung a sip of gall', students should inspect Clarke's intention. Is it merely meant to shock or does it also engender a strong and powerful comment in its process? Why might Clarke want to shock? What effect is she trying to nurture?

Activity 4 This activity allows students to explore Clarke's assertions that such disasters also tragically have an impact on the innocent.

One's hopes lie with the young. Is Clarke suggesting that man-made disasters are impacting on future well-being, regeneration and innocence? By contrasting the man-made disaster with the loss of innocence and innocent life, does the political and human concern and comment become intensified? Encourage students to examine these quotes and their meaning.

Activity 5 This activity asks students to examine a metaphor in the poem.

The word 'toxin' comes from the Greek word 'toxikon', meaning 'arrow poison'. The term was introduced into medicine in 1888 by the Berlin physician Brieger as a name for poisons made by infectious agents. In this metaphor, Clarke is making reference to the carried/transported toxins generated from this disaster, hitting the community and cattle like a poisoned arrow. A poisoned arrow traditionally brings pain and misery: this example only strengthens this concept.

Activity 6 This activity focuses students' attention on Clarke's use of alliteration.

Responses to this question will depend on the examples chosen by the students. Be sure that students provide appropriate examples of alliteration, as well as expressing the purpose of each. Some examples include:

- 'song-thrushes/steering north, smudged signatures on light'
- 'a mouthful of bitter air from the Ukraine/ brought by the wind out of its box of sorrows'.

Activity 7 This activity asks students to explain the dual reference to the colour blue in the last line, encouraging discussion and debate.

Take all valid answers. Could the waiting and watching refer to the fact that the farmers and the farming community in Wales are waiting in hope that their cattle do not contract the blue tongue disease?

Activity 8 This activity asks students to look at the poem's tone.

The rank ordering is dependent on student interpretation. However, consider the point that Clarke is using the poem as a vehicle to highlight her anger and worry regarding this human disaster: *anger* at the tragic and far-reaching consequences on man, flora and fauna and *worry* about the unknown impact and effects yet to be uncovered. Any valid and justified answer will suffice.

Structure and form

Activity 9 This activity looks at repetition in the poem.

The first part to this answer requires students to focus on Clarke's repetition of the word 'each'. Possible responses might suggest 'each' meaning 'every' – highlighting the enormity of the disaster. Likewise, Clarke may be taking into account injury and impact on a particularised level – never losing sight of the individual. Further and wider responses from the students should be encouraged, but likewise be justified and explained. Some other examples include 'late', 'lamb', and 'spring'.

Activity 10 This activity focuses on the narrative voice in the poem.

Ask pupils to consider the possibility that by using the first person plural 'we' instead of the first person singular 'I', Clarke further emphasises the fact that such global, man-made disasters have wide-reaching waves. Is Clarke also calling for people and communities to come together and voice their concerns? Is she using 'we' to unite reader and poet?

Activity 11 This activity asks students to comment on tense within the poem with particular reference to the changed 'we watched ...' (past tense) to 'we watch ...' (present tense).

Some suggestions for this might be that Clarke is emphasising how the problems and consequences of this disaster have not ceased. Indeed, years on,

communities, flora and fauna are still affected. (Refer students back to page 71 in the Student Book that draws their attention to the fact that some British farmers are still under restrictions over twenty years on). Use of the present tense places this disaster in the 'now': ongoing and ever present.

Stretch yourself This activity enables students to revisit their definition of 'neighbour' in light of their analysis.

Allow students the time to look this term up in a dictionary. Students will in turn explore the title and the heavy irony Clarke shrouds it in. Implications of what the geography of 'being a neighbour' means should be considered by the students – thinking more on a global level. Does Clarke think this global change and growing sense of global community is a good thing? What words might students use instead of 'neighbour'? Does Clarke feel that care and consideration and 'neighbourly' conduct was the backdrop to the Chernobyl disaster? Who might Clarke blame? Use this activity to examine and explore some of the deeper layers of meaning in this poem.

Students are reminded that they looked at titles and what they can tell the reader about a poem's meaning in Chapter 2.

Personal response

Activity 12 This activity requires a personal response from the students while facilitating deep thinking.

Students will use Clarke's details of impact and effect to imagine and understand the far-reaching and ongoing consequences of this disaster.

Comparing poems in the 'Place' cluster

Planning activity: Comparing MacCaig and Wordsworth

At the end of this chapter, students are provided with some guidance on how to approach the comparison element of the Anthology examination question (Unit 2A). In the exam, students will be asked to analyse a set poem from the 'Place' cluster; this could be any poem from the cluster so it is important that students are prepared to respond confidently to all of the poems in this cluster. Students will also be asked to analyse one other poem of their choice from the cluster in light of the focus of the question. For example, students may be asked:

Compare how nature is presented in 'Spellbound' and one other poem from the 'Place' cluster.

Analysing the question

It is of vital importance that students understand what is being asked of them in the exam. A sample question is annotated in the Student Book with the five key elements that students are required to address:

1 A **comparison** must be made

2 The poet's **techniques** must be examined

3 The **focus area** must be clear in students' minds

4 The **named poem** must be covered in the students' response

5 One **other** poem must be included in the analysis.

Activity 1 This activity asks students to annotate further sample questions in the same way to consolidate their writing.

Choosing your comparison poem

Remind students that the choice they make regarding the second poem they are able to analyse is crucial. They need to select a poem that will provide them with enough material to enable them to make a full and effective comparison, both in terms of the similarities between the poems and also the differences between them. Students should be able to compare:

- the attitudes and ideas presented
- the language and imagery used
- the structure and form of the poems.

Students have been working through the poems presented in this chapter according to these areas of analysis. The chapters of Section A, where these different aspects are individually introduced and explored, will provide further assurance for students wishing to revise the sort of techniques and devices they should be looking out for.

In planning their response, students are encouraged to record their initial ideas in a grid. This will help to direct their thoughts and discourage them from straying from the focus of the question. It will also enable them to see the similarities and differences between the two poems. The grid provided uses 'Spellbound' as an example.

Activity 2 This activity asks students to complete their own grid using an alternative comparison poem of their choice. This should illustrate to students that a variety of poems can be chosen for comparison – but that some choices are more effective than others.

This activity is replicated on Worksheet 8f in the online resources.

Structuring your answer

Once students are clear about what they need to do and the points they wish to cover, they can think about their opening paragraph. Encourage students to use this paragraph both for their own reference to outline what they intend to cover in their essay, and to ensure that they are clearly establishing the focus of their response for the examiner. This paragraph should immediately demonstrate skills of comparison. A sample paragraph is provided.

Activity 3 This activity asks students to write their own opening paragraph for their chosen comparison.

Students are then advised to draw on discourse markers to illustrate points of comparison in the main section of their response.

It is worth reinforcing at this stage that students should remember to consider the differences and contrasts between poems in addition to examining the similarities between them.

Activity 4 This activity asks students to write a paragraph in which they develop their comparison with the poem of their choice and underline the words that indicate that a comparison is being made. This should reinforce with students the need to constantly compare one poem with the other.

Reinforce with students the need to explain **how** and **why** a poet is creating certain effects rather than simply recounting which devices a poet has used. Also encourage students to make a personal response; examiners will be looking for evidence of engagement with the text.

Students are finally advised to make an insightful comment in their closing paragraph to illustrate that they are comparing the poems to the end of their essay.

Activity 5 This activity asks students to write their final paragraph and to include their final pertinent point.

Students could contribute alternative questions to help them to become comfortable with the structure of the question. This would encourage them to think about potential pairings of poems in readiness for the exam.

Remind students to bear in mind the theme of 'Place' throughout their analysis. What do the poems they are writing about offer in an exploration of this theme?

Outcomes

kt Interactive activity: Reflecting on the 'Place' cluster

In this chapter students have learned how to:

- approach analysing poems in the 'Place' cluster
- compare two poems in the cluster.

AO focus

AO1: Respond to texts critically and imaginatively; select and evaluate relevant textual detail to illustrate and support interpretation.

AO2: Explain how language, structure and form contribute to writers' presentation of ideas, themes and settings.

AO3: Make comparisons and explain links between texts, evaluating writers' different ways of expressing meaning and achieving effects.

In this chapter your students will:

- explore the theme of conflict in poetry
- analyse and comment on the meaning, language, imagery, structure and form of a selection of poems from the 'Conflict' cluster of their Anthology through close reading and investigation activities
- explain poems in relation to social, cultural and historical settings
- strengthen their own understanding and use of poetic terms
- gain confidence in making a personal response to the poems they read.

In this chapter, students analyse a sample selection of the poems from the 'Conflict' cluster of the Anthology. The key aspects of analysis that students covered in Section A of the Student Book: meaning (Chapter 1), language (Chapter 2), imagery (Chapter 3), structure (Chapter 4) and verse form (Chapter 5), now shape the progression of activities in Section B, so that for each poem in turn, students are asked to answer questions on meaning, language and imagery, structure and form and personal response. The addition of personal response here reflects the need for students to engage with texts on an individual level – something examiners will be looking for evidence of. It is hoped that this consistent and logical approach will help to demystify the study of poetry and increase students' confidence by equipping them with a clear method with which to apply their skills of analysis.

Key terms

Key terms the students are introduced to in this chapter:

- Monologue
- Persona

Poems included in this chapter

Six of the poems from this cluster are covered in the Student Book, the remainder are covered in the online resources. The poems covered in the Student Book are written by a range of male and female poets, both contemporary and from the Literary Heritage. All of the poems in this chapter are suitable for students studying both Foundation and Higher Tiers.

Poems covered in this chapter:

- 'Flag' by John Agard
- 'Futility' by Wilfred Owen
- 'Mametz Wood' by Owen Sheers
- 'The Charge of the Light Brigade' by Alfred, Lord Tennyson
- 'Belfast Confetti' by Ciaran Carson
- 'Hawk Roosting' by Ted Hughes

Poems in the 'Conflict' cluster covered in the online resources:

- Analysis activity: 'You have picked me out'
- Viewpoints activity: 'The Yellow Palm'
- Interactive activity: Responding to 'The Right Word'
- Interactive activity: 'Falling Leaves'
- Interactive activity: 'Come on, come back'
- Interactive activity: Responding to 'Bayonet Charge'
- Analysis activity: 'next to god of course america'

Additional resources

Worksheets:

- 9a: 'Futility' Activity 3
- 9b: The Charge of the Light Brigade Activity 2
- 9c: Choosing your comparison poem

Audio recordings of some of the poems used in this chapter are also available in the online resources, including some alternative readings.

Getting started

The theme of conflict is introduced here to encourage students to think about why this is an area that poets choose to write on. They are invited to think about the different types of conflict and the emotional effect they can have. Most students will immediately think of war and battles when considering what poetry about conflict may consist of, but the introduction to the chapter encourages them to think of other instances of conflict too. The poems that are covered in this chapter explore the effect that different types of conflict can have on us and the emotional struggle that results. At the beginning of the activities for each poem, the theme of conflict is reinforced and students are encouraged to think about why each particular poem appears in this cluster and what it has to offer in an exploration of this theme.

Throughout the chapter, students are reminded that they should always consider the theme of this cluster and think about what the individual poets are saying about relationships in each of the poems. The activities, therefore, continually link back to this theme while exploring different aspects of analysis.

Activity This introductory activity is designed to get students thinking and talking about the word 'conflict'. Before they analyse the poems in this cluster, it is important that they have an understanding that conflict is not just about war. Challenge students to think about the many forms, causes and victims of conflict as well as how people may respond.

Working through the chapter

Background information is given for each of the six poems in this chapter. Some biographical information is given about each poet and some introductory information about each poem is provided so that students can contextualise poems before embarking on a full analysis.

Of course, you may not have time in the classroom to explore each of the poems in the cluster in as much detail as is explored in the Student Book. The material that is presented here is intended as a suggested 'ideal' model of approach but you may only be able to select certain areas to focus on. It is hoped that you will be able to apply some, if not all, of this approach. However, it is by no means prescriptive and should not be interpreted as the number of activities that students will 'need' to have completed in preparation for their exam.

The personal response activities are crucial but by their nature are problematic to assess. For these activities, some guidance regarding the sort of response students are likely to submit is given, but this by no means should be taken as 'correct'. Students should be encouraged to engage with the poems on a personal level and to feel confident in voicing their interpretations as long as they can be supported with evidence from the poem text.

Before the poems are looked at in detail, students could be reminded of the guidance on how to read a poem, guidance they met in the Section A introduction. This summarises all the key areas that they should pay attention to as they read the Anthology poems for the first time.

'Flag' by John Agard

This poem is suitable for students entered for Foundation Tier. It explores the symbolism of flags by looking beyond what they look like and considering what they stand for.

Meaning

Activity 1 This activity provides a way of clarifying that students understand the introduction to the poem and can therefore articulate what flags are used for and can state the many places that you may find them, for example courthouses, schools, hotels, etc. You may wish to explore terms such as: 'identity' and 'inclusion' in relation to flags that represent football clubs or other sporting or musical groups. Terms such as 'patriotism' may also need to be explored at this point.

Activity 2 This activity asks students to focus on the tone of the poem.

Students may suggest points such as: the repetition suggests a cynical tone as 'a piece of cloth' can be very dangerous. Agard is highlighting the difference between what a flag literally is and what it symbolically represents.

The words that fit best are: cynical, negative, angry and bitter.

Activity 3 This activity asks students to explore 'Then blind your conscience to the end.'

Agard appears to be suggesting that if you own a flag, people often become blind to the horrors that they can lead to. They are 'blinded' by patriotism and the positive imagery associated with flags and they do not consider how they 'outlive the blood you bleed' or how they can bring 'a nation to its knees.'

Language and imagery

Activity 4 This activity asks students to consider Agard's use of contrasting language.

There are a few different possibilities here but one may be:

'It's just a piece of cloth
that will outlive the blood you bleed.'

Students should pick on the graphic and violent language of 'blood' and 'bleed' which are quite shocking. Also, the active word 'outlive' suggests that flags will last longer than people, which again makes the reader think about flags and what they can symbolise. This strengthens the irony of the word 'just'.

Activity 5 This activity focuses students' attention on the violent language in the poem.

Graphic language such as 'guts', 'blood', 'bleed' and 'to its knees' make the lines powerful. They remind the reader that conflict can have fatal and devastating consequences that can affect many people in different ways.

Activity 6 This activity asks students to choose an interpretation of Agard's repetition.

Students should select 'It highlights that there is more to flags than meets the eye.' In the final stanza the focus is on how to get a flag and the fact that you would need to abandon your conscience to get it. The emphasis has changed from the effects of flags to the means to obtain one.

Activity 7 This activity focuses students' attention on the imagery in the poem.

This largely requires a personal response but an example might be: 'Agard states in the second stanza that a flag 'makes the guts of men grow bold'. The reference to 'guts' is quite shocking and the fact that Agard refers to the men's guts as growing bold suggests almost a false or futile pride and confidence. This could be linked to emotions such as patriotism.' This activity will enable students to practise writing full comments about the effects of particular poetic techniques.

Structure and form

Activity 8 This activity asks students to look at the poem's structure.

Students should consider how stanzas 1–4 start with a question which is followed by the repeated phrase 'It's just a piece of cloth', which in turn is followed by a negative image of the destruction that flags can bring about. The repetitive structure reflects the many negative elements to flags that Agard wants to highlight. The final verse is different in structure as the question is about how to obtain a flag and therefore the next two lines answer that question. Agard is suggesting that to own a flag you have to 'blind' your conscience to the true horrors that can often hide behind these patriotic symbols.

Students are reminded that they looked at stanzas of different lengths in Chapter 4.

Activity 9 This activity asks students to consider Agard's use of questions.

a The questions make the reader think about the places flags fly. However, the seemingly innocent questions are contrasted by the harsh reality of what the 'piece of cloth' can result in.

b Agard has placed the questions at the start of each stanza as the rest of the stanza answers the question. Also, the contrast between the question and the harsh answer that follows shocks the reader and therefore creates maximum impact.

Activity 10 This activity asks students to think about the poem's rhyme scheme.

Students should comment on how the last words on lines 1 and 3 rhyme in stanzas 1–4 but the rhyme pattern changes in stanza 5. Discuss why the rhyme pattern changes; for example, Agard wanted to emphasise the last two lines as 'friend' and 'end' are a powerful conclusion to the poem. The poem sounds like a conversation as you read it.

Activity 11 This activity asks students to consider the effect of Agard's use of enjambement.

Enjambement enables the poet to repeat and therefore emphasise 'It's just a piece of cloth/that' which is the key to the poet's frustration – how can a piece of cloth lead to such conflict? It also means that the reader is anticipating the answer which always starts with 'that'. The enjambement also symbolises the freedom of the flag flying and the fact that conflict is not governed by rules.

Students are reminded that they looked at enjambement and its effect in Chapter 5.

Personal response

Activity 12 This activity requires a personal response from students.

Ask students if their attitude towards flags has changed after reading 'Flag'. Has it enabled them to view flags and conflict in a different light?

'Futility' by Wilfred Owen

This poem is suitable for students entered for both Foundation and Higher Tiers. It explores the tragedy of conflict by depicting a young soldier's desperation to save his comrade and friend.

Meaning

Activity 1 This activity asks students to explore the title of the poem.

They may want to research dictionary definitions and create synonyms for 'futility'. Following this, students should have a go at making a prediction about the poem's content.

Students are reminded that they looked at poem titles in Chapter 2.

Activity 2 This activity is intended to help students get to grips with the historical context of the poem.

The number of soldiers that died in the First World War is over 700,000. Discuss this with the class. How does this figure make them feel? Are they shocked by it?

Activity 3 This activity reinforces with students the need to substantiate their views with evidence from the poem.

Here some suggested answers but obviously valid alternatives should be accepted.

Evidence	Comment
'Move him into the sun'	'him' is a reference to a dead soldier. At a simple level Owen is commenting on how the sun used to wake him in a morning and maybe now it will stir him again.
'whispering of fields unsown'	This is a reference to work that may have needed to be done when the soldier was at home.
'If anything might rouse him now'	Owen knows really that nothing will rouse him but the statement shows Owen's sorrow at the loss.
'Is it for this the clay grew tall?'	Owen questions why the emergence of human life evolved from clay at all when it can so easily be destroyed.
'O what made fatuous sunbeams toil/To break earth's sleep at all?'	Owen questions why the sun worked hard to create life if it is destroyed so easily. 'Fatuous' shows his anger.

This activity is replicated on Worksheet 9a in the online resources.

Activity 4 This activity focuses students' attention on Owen's choice of language to depict his feelings.

Students should annotate the second stanza to show words or phrases illustrating Owen's anger/indignation. Below are some suggestions but valid alternatives should be accepted.

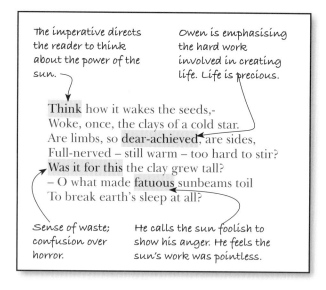

The imperative directs the reader to think about the power of the sun.

Owen is emphasising the hard work involved in creating life. Life is precious.

Think how it wakes the seeds,-
Woke, once, the clays of a cold star.
Are limbs, so dear-achieved, are sides,
Full-nerved – still warm – too hard to stir?
Was it for this the clay grew tall?
– O what made fatuous sunbeams toil
To break earth's sleep at all?

Sense of waste; confusion over horror.

He calls the sun foolish to show his anger. He feels the sun's work was pointless.

Activity 5 This activity follows on from Activity 4 in focusing students on Owen's anger.

Owen also shows his anger in the second stanza through his use of questions. He is outraged and in disbelief that such a tragic loss of life has been allowed to happen.

Language and imagery

Activity 6 This activity looks at the sun imagery in the poem.

a The sun is seen as kind and a provider of light and warmth. The following quotes are examples which support this:

- 'gently its touch …'
- 'the kind old sun …'
- 'it wakes the seeds'.

b Owen is expressing his anger that the sun toiled to create human life but it was all a wasted effort as men can so easily destroy each other. The sun, in giving life, light and warmth, is in stark contrast to war, which destroys life. The spider diagram on conflict should communicate Owen's anger at the waste. He thinks the work of the sun to create life was futile.

The following points could be made in students' spider diagrams:

- 'even in France' – the soldiers are in a foreign country away from home.
- 'this snow' – contrasts with warmth of the sun.
- '… too hard to stir?' – the dead bodies contrast with the life the sun can help to create.

Activity 7 This activity asks students to examine Owen's imagery in the second stanza.

a Owen is saying that the effects of conflict are lasting. The injuries/deaths cannot be reversed. He cannot believe that life can be so quickly and easily taken away.

b The clay Owen refers to is the earth. Owen alludes to the fact that this is what we are returned to as a result of conflict.

Structure and form

Activity 8 This activity asks students to select an interpretation of Owen's choice of structure.

This requires a personal response to some extent but students may want to consider the link with the title. Owen feels it is pointless to say too much. He has made his point in a succinct way that has maximum impact.

Activity 9 This activity focuses students' attention on the last two lines of the poem.

Owen ends on a question to show his despair at the waste. He wants his readers to see the contrast between how hard the sun worked to create life and how easily it can be taken away. The question highlights his incomprehension at the horror.

Personal response

Activity 10 This activity requires a personal response.

Once students have written their paragraphs, you may wish to ask some to share their response with the class.

'Mametz Wood' by Owen Sheers

This poem is suitable for students entered for both Foundation and Higher Tiers. It explores the poet's response on witnessing the unearthing of the remains of Welsh soldiers at Mametz Wood.

The Poetry Archive has a recording of Sheers talking about the poem and reading it at www. poetryarchive.org but students may also be interested to find out more about the location of Mametz Wood. A KWL grid could be used to help students to structure their findings.

Meaning

Activity 1 This activity asks students to look at why the passage of time is presented in this poem.

Sheers wants to draw attention to the passing of time as he is trying to show that the devastating effects of conflict can still shock and upset people many years after the original event.

Activity 2 This activity asks students to analyse the simile 'like a wound working a foreign body to the surface of the skin'.

This is a graphic image which makes the reader think of how the skin repairs itself by forcing out

foreign bodies such as glass or wood splinters. The land is forcing out the remains of the soldiers as they too do not belong there. Also, the death of these young men was a devastating loss that should not just be forgotten.

Activity 3 This activity asks students to discuss the tone of the poem.

Students are likely to suggest that the tone of the poem is sad. Sheers thinks it is an enormous waste of life. It also reminds us of how vulnerable men at war actually are.

Stretch yourself This activity asks students to write a newspaper article about the finding at Mametz Wood. This will enable students to write creatively and to think about what information they learn from the poem.

Language and imagery

Activity 4 This activity directs students to Sheers' use of language and asks them to select an example and comment on its effect.

Here are some suggestions:

- 'the earth stands sentinel' suggests the earth is on guard possibly searching for new discoveries. It creates an eerie and sombre mood.

- 'a broken mosaic of bone' is striking as bones should be structured. The bone breaks the pattern due to injuries and the fact that the bodies have decomposed. The word usually associated with art seems out of place and somewhat macabre. Again, it is a shocking image for the reader.

- 'their socketed heads tilted back at an angle' is a graphic image which focuses on how the bodies had decomposed. This image recreates some of the shock that Sheers must have felt.

Activity 5 This activity asks students to comment on Sheers's use of metaphor.

An example of a metaphor in this poem is 'breaking blue in white/across this field'. This metaphor highlights how the remains of the soldiers are turning up at the site like china being discovered at an archaeological dig. Likening the bone to china stresses its fragility and seems to trivialise the memory of the soldiers. Sheers wants to remind us of this event – which seems to have been forgotten – and to highlight the scale of the loss.

Structure and form

Activity 6 This activity asks students to think about the use of enjambement in the poem and how this technique might allow Sheers to make a comment about conflict.

Sheers has stated in interviews that he mostly writes for the ear and enjambement creates audible interest. He believes that not all thoughts are the same length and enjambement helps the flow of the narrative because it is more natural. The enjambement in this poem could also reflect the fact that conflict does not have any rules, constraints or set structure. Conflict can last for different periods of time and can have different consequences.

Activity 7 This activity asks students to select a reason why Sheers has not used a rhyme scheme.

Students may suggest that it is more natural not to have rhyme to recount what Sheers witnessed as he was saddened by the remains of the soldiers and did not therefore want to make the poem sound too lyrical – although any of the possible interpretations can be supported. Ask students if they think the rhyme in the last verse is significant. Did Sheers want to emphasise the ending? Does it give it more finality?

Personal response

Activity 8 This activity requires a personal response from students. It is intended to help students think of pertinent questions to aid their analysis and appreciation of a poem.

Activity 9 This activity also requires a personal response from students. Ask students to write a short paragraph in groups about Sheers's intentions and then present this to the class.

'The Charge of the Light Brigade' by Alfred, Lord Tennyson

This poem is suitable for students entered for both Foundation and Higher Tiers. It recounts a mistake made by an officer during the Crimean War which led to many soldiers losing their lives.

Meaning

Activity 1 This activity draws students' attention to the sense of drama created by Tennyson in the poem.

Students should make reference to:

- the repetition of 'half a league' which adds pace and anticipation as it mimics the rhythm of the horses
- the repetition of 'six hundred' as it is such a huge number of men
- 'the valley of Death' hints that men will lose their lives.

Activity 2 This activity asks students to think about the different emotions that the poem evokes.

a The table could be completed with the examples below. Focus students' attention on the sorrow and glory elements here as students have already covered the drama aspect in Activity 1.

	Evidence from the poem
Drama	• 'Cannon to right of them/Cannon to left of them …' • 'Half a league half a league,/Half a league onward' • 'Volley'd and thunder'd' • 'Into the jaws of Death,/Into the mouth of Hell' • 'Plunged in the battery-smoke/Right thro' the line they broke'
Sorrow	• 'While horse and hero fell' • 'Then they rode back, but not/Not the six hundred' • 'They that had fought so well' • 'Not tho' the soldier knew/Some one had blunder'd' • 'Theirs but to do and die'
Glory	• 'Boldly they rode and well' • 'When can their glory fade?' • 'Honour the charge they made!' • 'Flash'd as they turn'd in air' • 'All the world wonder'd'

b Tennyson is illustrating here that conflict can result in many different emotions. Discuss with the class what other emotional responses to conflict students can think of.

This activity is replicated on Worksheet 9b on the online resources.

Activity 3 This activity asks students to look closely at the text and to find examples of both celebration of the soldier's courage and the mourning of their loss.

There are alternative possibilities but here are a couple of examples:

- Courage of the men: 'Honour the Light Brigade,/Noble six hundred!'

Tennyson is almost commanding his readers to recognise the courage of the men and to honour their memory.

- Tragedy of the loss: 'Theirs not to make reply.'

The soldiers had to obey; they were not trained to question. There is an inherent sadness in this line as Tennyson makes clear that the soldiers had no choice but to charge to their deaths.

Stretch yourself This activity encourages students to write creatively and to imagine that they are a survivor of the charge. Remind students that they are attempting to think like a soldier from the time of the Crimean War and not like a soldier today. In order to do this, some students may want to research the historical context of the battle. You could display some examples from students on the wall.

Language and imagery

Activity 4 This activity asks students to consider the effect of Tennyson's use of repetition in the poem.

Some further examples of repetition include:

- 'Half a league' – which mimics the rhythm of the horses galloping
- 'the valley of Death' – which hints at disaster
- 'Rode the six hundred' – which emphasises the sheer number of men involved.

Students may find reading the poem aloud helpful here.

Activity 5 This activity focuses on Tennyson's use of verbs in the poem.

The rank ordering will be personal opinion but some of the verbs that students may discuss are:

- 'volley'd'
- 'thunder'd'
- 'stormed'
- 'charging'
- 'rode'.

Discuss with the class how the frequent use of verbs conveys the sense of movement and action and heightens the drama in the poem.

Activity 6 This activity asks students to consider the use of metaphor in the poem.

The metaphors used by Tennyson emphasise the danger that the men rode into and shock the reader with their forcefulness and violent connotations. 'Death' and 'hell' hint that the men would not come out alive.

Structure and form

Activity 7 This activity asks students to think about Tennyson's final question in the poem.

'When can their glory fade?' suggests that they should never be forgotten and that their glory will never diminish as they were so brave and loyal. Discuss with students why Tennyson has placed this question at the beginning of the last stanza – to remind them of the importance of word placement.

Activity 8 This activity focuses students' attention on the rhyme-scheme.

The rhyme is not in a regular pattern but the middle sections of stanzas 2–5 rhyme, which speeds up the action that is being narrated and builds the excitement and tension (this is also heightened by the use of short lines). This is particularly clear when the poem is read aloud; ask students to read aloud in pairs so that they notice the change in pace.

Personal response

Activity 9 This activity requires a personal response but many students may comment that conflict has been an enduring part of human existence over the ages and that every instance of conflict can result in tragic losses. The pain and suffering of the soldiers and their loved ones is as potent in an ancient battle as it is in modern warfare. Students may feel that Tennyson's poem still has something to offer in that it focuses on the glory of the soldiers – something that is often deliberately left out of the more disillusioned war poetry of the First and Second World Wars.

'Belfast Confetti' by Ciaran Carson

This poem is suitable for students entered for Higher Tier. It explores a bombing of Belfast city centre and the ensuing confusion.

Meaning

Activity 1 This activity is an introductory activity is intended to help students think about the title of the poem and to access its content.

Students will have differing levels of knowledge about the conflict in Belfast. You may like to spend some time with your students researching the history of the city and in discovering why conflict has occurred there. While completing their spider diagram about confetti, students should focus on the emotional connotations of weddings and think about how this contrasts with the feelings that can result from conflict.

Activity 2 This activity asks students to look at how the poet communicates his feelings about the explosion in a specified part of the poem.

In their paragraph, students should focus on Carson's confusion. He is bewildered by the blast and has lost his bearings – the streets he knows so well have become a 'labyrinth' to him. He is distressed because he cannot find an escape route from the carnage, the streets are 'blocked'. He is shocked and unable to communicate properly, 'I was trying to complete a sentence'. The references to punctuation marks illustrate his confusion further – he is desperate to make sense of this event, but he is 'stuttering'.

Activity 3 This activity also asks students to think about how Carson expresses his shock in the opening of the poem.

Students could select any of the following:

- It is 'raining exclamation marks' – the exclamation mark is used in writing to express shock or surprise. The sharp shape of this mark also lends itself well to the image of rain.
- The list of 'nuts, bolts, nails, car-keys' – the list of these hard, metallic objects highlights the extent of the blast and the devastation and fear it is causing.
- There is no full stop after 'And the explosion' – the use of enjambement here shows Carson's shock and the impact of the explosion.

Activity 4 This activity asks students to think again about the poem's title now that they have studied the poem in more detail.

The title is ironic as confetti is usually associated with weddings, which are a loving celebration.

Stretch yourself This activity is intended to help students get to grips with the content of the poem and to think about how an eye-witness account could be created from the information presented. Encourage students to focus on how Carson feels about the explosion.

This activity should help students to see the difference between prose and verse forms and to experiment with the limitations and opportunities of the two in terms of communicating emotion.

Language and imagery

Activity 5 This activity asks students to look at the potentially unfamiliar vocabulary in the poem.

Students could suggest that Carson may have used unfamiliar language intentionally to replicate the confusion in the poem. A lot of the vocabulary concerns violence, weaponry and famous battle names. This heightens the sense of threat that permeates the poem.

Activity 6 This activity asks students to look at how Carson has used the imagery of punctuation in the poem.

One example here could be: 'And the/explosion/ Itself – an asterisk on the map.' From above, an explosion may look like a large asterisk. Of course, it may also be a real asterisk on a map when police locate the scene.

Activity 7 This activity further looks at the symbolism of the punctuation marks in the poem.

Students could make the following points about communication in their spider diagram:

- brings people together
- promotes understanding
- helps to resolve issues.

Carson is using punctuation marks, symbols of communication, to create a powerful contrast with the breakdown in communication which can lead to such terrible conflict. This highlights the difference between something which brings people together and enhances understanding, and something that breaks people apart and causes distress and pain.

Structure and form

Activity 8 This activity focuses students' attention on the form of the poem.

a The individual lines and stanzas are of differing lengths and there is no regular form to this poem. This reflects Carson's confusion and disorientation after the explosion. Nothing is set or ordered, everything has been shaken out of place.

b The poem looks like confetti randomly scattered on the page.

Activity 9 This activity looks at Carson's use of questions in the poem.

a Students should identify the final bullet point; that conflict has a major effect on the identity of ordinary people. The results of conflict can be so extreme that the lives of innocent victims are thrown into turmoil and can have irreversible results. The three questions Carson uses, 'What is my name? Where am I coming from? Where am I going?' are all fundamental questions which should incite very simple responses. This highlights the extent of the damage that can be inflicted.

b Carson uses 'I' and 'me' to show the personal impact conflict can have. He uses these words at this point in the poem to assert his own identity which is under threat.

Activity 10 This activity asks students to consider Carson's use of enjambement in the poem.

Enjambement is used to reflect the chaotic nature of the explosion. It is on-going and unpredictable. Another example is 'What is/My name?'

Activity 11 This activity asks students to think about the lack of rhyme-scheme in the poem.

The lack of rhyme reflects how conflict is unpredictable and shocking. To impose a flowing rhyme-scheme here would seem false and detract from Carson's intention.

Personal response

Activity 12 This activity requires a personal response. Students could select any one of the adjectives given as all can be supported. You could collate the response from the class and ask if students can come up with any additional adjectives to describe how the poem makes them feel.

'Hawk Roosting' by Ted Hughes

This poem is suitable for students entered for both Foundation and Higher Tiers. It is presented from the point of view of a hawk.

Meaning

Activity 1 This activity asks students to compile a list of adjectives that describe a hawk.

This activity is intended to help students get to grips with the subject matter of the poem before they begin their analysis. Collate responses from the class. Are there any adjectives that some students disagree with? You could place an image of a hawk on the board to facilitate their discussion.

Activity 2 This activity asks students to create a spider diagram of their first impressions of the hawk after reading the poem.

This activity largely requires a personal response but students may be directed to the violence, arrogance and superiority of the hawk, which they may not have thought about in Activity 1. Does this depiction of the hawk shock them at all? Did they like or dislike the hawk as they read the poem?

Activity 3 This activity focuses students' attention on the language Hughes uses to express the superiority of the hawk.

Some suggestions to show the hawk thinks it is superior are:

- 'I sit in the top of the wood,'
- 'Now I hold Creation in my foot'
- 'I kill where I please because it is all mine.'

Activity 4 This activity asks students to focus on a stanza and annotate it. They are then asked to write a paragraph explaining the impression of the hawk.

An example of another annotated stanza is as follows:

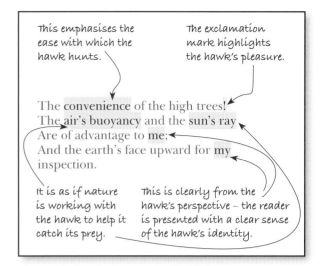

This emphasises the ease with which the hawk hunts.

The exclamation mark highlights the hawk's pleasure.

The convenience of the high trees!
The air's buoyancy and the sun's ray
Are of advantage to me;
And the earth's face upward for my inspection.

It is as if nature is working with the hawk to help it catch its prey.

This is clearly from the hawk's perspective – the reader is presented with a clear sense of the hawk's identity.

In this stanza, Hughes is further enforcing the hawk's dominance. Nature seems to be complying with the hawk so that it is able to hunt easily and assert its authority. Hughes emphasises the 'convenience' of the elements of nature that the hawk is able to use to its advantage. The repeated use of personal pronouns highlights the perspective of the poem and reinforces the hawk's strength and prowess.

Language and imagery

Activity 5 This activity directs students to think about the tone of the poem.

The following are examples of quotations that support each selection:

- Frightening: 'I sit in the top of the wood, my eyes closed'.
- Dangerous: 'Between my hooked head and hooked feet'.
- Violent: 'My manners are tearing off heads'.
- Arrogant: 'I kill where I please because it is all mine'.
- Threatening: 'For the one path of my flight is direct'.

The tone could also be described as superior, cold and calculating.

Activity 6 This activity asks students to think about the violent imagery in the poem.

a An example response from students could be:

'My feet are locked upon the rough bark': this tells the reader that the hawk is very resilient and powerful as it is perched on the 'rough bark'. Its strength is conveyed by the use of the word 'locked'. This generates a threatening and commanding image of the hawk.

b Students should select either the first or third bullet point. Encourage students to support their interpretation with evidence from the text.

Structure and form

Activity 7 This activity asks students to consider why Hughes has chosen to adopt the monologue form.

The term monologue is defined in the Student Book but some students may need further explanation; the material on Robert Browning's 'My Last Duchess' in Chapter 10 of the Student Book could be a useful starting point.

The monologue form here allows Hughes to truly infiltrate the psyche of the hawk by creating a very personal and direct form of narration. The reader can fully access the perspective of the hawk and see the world through its eyes. The monologue gives a strong voice to the persona and this is exactly the type of voice Hughes wants to give the hawk.

Activity 8 This activity focuses students' attention on Hughes's choice of persona in the poem.

The term persona is defined in the Student Book but some students may need further explanation; the opening of Chapter 7, where different types of narrative voice are introduced, could be a useful starting point.

By adopting this persona, Hughes is able to get into the mindset of the hawk and get closer to its motivations and desires than if he had adopted a human voice.

Activity 9 This activity asks students to comment on the lack of rhyme scheme in the poem.

Students could respond that a rhyme scheme may have lent a falsely lyrical quality to the poem. The poem is essentially about the violent force of nature, and a regular rhyme scheme would not be reflective of the chaotic destruction that takes place in the wild.

Personal response

Activity 10 This activity requires a personal response from students although they are likely to say that they are intimidated by the hawk. Discuss with students whether Hughes could be intending his readers to feel like the hawk's prey. Do they feel this way at all?

Activity 11 This activity asks students to compare the hawk with a despotic and tyrannical character like Adolf Hitler.

Students may make connections between Hitler and the hawk through lines such as:

- 'in sleep rehearse perfect kills'
- 'I hold creation in my foot'

- 'I kill where I please'
- 'No arguments assert my right'
- 'I am going to keep things like this.'

Do students feel that this is an accurate comparison to make? Are there any other people the hawk could be likened to?

Stretch yourself This activity is intended to encourage students to think creatively about narrative voice. It will also help them to think carefully about the effects of different language. Encourage them to think about vocabulary and imagery that creates a sense of power and strength. You could make a display of students' final poems around a copy of 'Hawk Roosting'.

Comparing poems in the 'Conflict' cluster

kt) Viewpoints activity: Comparing 'At the border' with 'Cameo Appearance'

kt) Analysis activity: Comparing your choice of poems from the cluster

At the end of this chapter, students are provided with some guidance as to how to approach the comparison element of the Anthology examination question (Unit 2A). In the exam, students will be asked to analyse a set poem from the 'Conflict' cluster; this could be any poem from the cluster so it is important that students are prepared to respond confidently to all of the poems in this cluster. Students will also be asked to analyse one other poem of their choice from the cluster in light of the focus of the question. For example, students may be asked:

> Compare attitudes to war in 'The Charge of the Light Brigade' and one other poem from the 'Conflict' cluster.

Analysing the question

It is of vital importance that students understand what is being asked of them in the exam. A sample question is annotated in the Student Book with the five key elements that students are required to address:

1 A **comparison** must be made

2 The poet's **techniques** must be examined

3 The **focus area** must be clear in student's minds

4 The **named poem** must be covered in the student's response

5 **One other** poem must be included in the analysis.

Activity 1 This activity asks students to annotate further sample questions in the same way to consolidate their learning.

Choosing your comparison poem

Remind students that the choice they make regarding the second poem they shall analyse is crucial. They need to select a poem that will provide them with enough material to make a full and effective comparison, both in terms of the similarities between the poems and also the differences between them. Students should be able to compare:

- the attitudes and ideas presented
- the language and imagery used
- the structure and form of the poems.

Students have been working through the poems presented in this chapter according to these areas of analysis. The chapters of Section A, where these different aspects are individually introduced and explored, will provide further assurance for students wishing to revise the sort of techniques and devices they should be looking out for.

In planning their response, students are encouraged to record their initial ideas in a grid. This will help to direct their thoughts and discourage them from straying from the focus of the question. It will also enable them to see the similarities and differences between the two poems. The grid provided uses 'Mametz Wood' as an example.

Activity 2 This activity asks students to complete their own grid using an alternative comparison poem of their choice. This should illustrate to students that a variety of poems can be chosen for comparison – but that some choices are more effective than others.

This activity is replicated on Worksheet 9c in the online resources.

Structuring your answer

Once students are clear about what they need to do and the points they wish to cover, they can think about their opening paragraph. Encourage students to use this paragraph both for their own reference (to outline what they intend to cover in their essay) and to ensure that they are clearly establishing the focus of their response for the examiner. This paragraph should immediately demonstrate skills of comparison. A sample paragraph is provided.

Activity 3 This activity asks students to write their own opening paragraph for their chosen comparison. Students are then advised to draw on discourse markers to illustrate points of comparison in the main section of their response.

It is worth reinforcing at this stage that students should remember to consider the differences and contrasts between poems in addition to examining the similarities between them.

Activity 4 This activity asks students to write a paragraph in which they develop their comparison with the poem of their choice and underline the words that indicate that a comparison is being made. This should reinforce with students the need to constantly compare one poem with the other.

Reinforce with students the need to explain **how** and **why** a poet is creating certain effects rather than simply recounting which devices a poet has used. Also encourage students to make a personal response; examiners will be looking for evidence of engagement with the text.

Students are finally advised to make an insightful comment in their closing paragraph to illustrate that they are comparing the poems to the end of their essay.

Activity 5 This activity asks students to write their final paragraph and to include their final pertinent point.

Students could contribute alternative questions to help them to become comfortable with the structure of the question. This would encourage them to think about potential pairings of poems in readiness for the exam.

Remind students to bear in mind the theme of 'Conflict' throughout their analysis. What do the poems they are writing about offer in an exploration of this theme?

Outcomes

Interactive activity: Multiple choice quiz on 'Conflict' cluster

In this chapter students have learned how to:

- approach analysing poems in the 'Conflict' cluster
- compare two poems in the cluster.

AO focus

AO1: Respond to texts critically and imaginatively; select and evaluate relevant textual detail to illustrate and support interpretation.

AO2: Explain how language, structure and form contribute to writers' presentation of ideas, themes and settings.

AO3: Make comparisons and explain links between texts, evaluating writers' different ways of expressing meaning and achieving effects.

In this chapter your students will:

- explore the theme of relationships in poetry
- analyse and comment on the meaning, language, imagery, structure and form a selection of poems from the 'Relationships' cluster of their Anthology through close reading and investigation activities
- explain poems in relation to social, cultural and historical settings
- strengthen their own understanding and use of poetic terms
- gain confidence in making a personal response to the poems they read.

In the course of the chapter, students analyse a sample selection of the poems from the 'Relationships' cluster of the Anthology. The key aspects of analysis that students covered in Section A of the Student Book: meaning (Chapter 1), language (Chapter 2), imagery (Chapter 3), structure (Chapter 4) and verse form (Chapter 5), now shape the progression of activities in Section B, so that for each poem in turn, students are asked to answer questions on meaning, language and imagery, structure and form and personal response. The addition of personal response here reflects the need for students to engage with texts on an individual level – something examiners will be looking for evidence of. It is hoped that this consistent and logical approach will help to demystify the study of poetry and increase students' confidence by equipping them with a clear method with which to apply their skills of analysis.

Key terms

Key terms the students are introduced to in this chapter:

- Symbol
- Personal pronoun
- Past tense
- Sonnet
- Persona
- Half rhyme

Poems included in this chapter

Six of the poems from this cluster are covered in the Student Book, the remainder are covered in the online resources. The poems covered in the Student Book are written by a range of male and female poets, both contemporary and from the Literary Heritage. All of the poems in this chapter are suitable for students studying both Foundation and Higher Tiers.

Poems covered in this chapter:

- 'Nettles' by Vernon Scannell
- 'Praise Song for my Mother' by Grace Nichols
- 'How Do I Love Thee?' by Elizabeth Barrett Browning
- 'To His Coy Mistress' by Andrew Marvell
- 'The Manhunt' by Simon Armitage
- 'Quickdraw' by Carol Ann Duffy

These poems from the 'Relationships' cluster are covered by online resources:

- Interactive activity: 'Ghazal' by Mimi Khalvati
- Interactive activity: Responding to 'The Engine' by Jean Sprackland
- Interactive activity: Responding to 'In Paris With You' by James Fenton
- Viewpoints activity: 'Harmonium' by Simon Armitage
- Analysis activity: Analysing 'Hour' by Carol Ann Duffy
- Interactive activity: Interpreting 'Let me not to the marriage of true minds' by William Shakespeare
- Analysis activity: Analysing 'Born Yesterday' by Philip Larkin
- Viewpoints activity: 'The Farmer's Bride' by Charlotte Mew

Additional resources

Worksheets:

- 10a: 'How Do I Love Thee?' Activity 1
- 10b: 'To His Coy Mistress' Activity 3
- 10c: 'The Manhunt' Activity 2

- 10d: 'Quickdraw' Activity 2
- 10e: 'Choosing your comparison poem

Audio recordings of some of the poems used in this chapter are also available in the online resources, including some alternative readings.

Getting started

The theme of relationships is introduced here to encourage students to think about why this is an area that poets choose to write about. They are invited to think about the different types of relationships and the emotional effect they can have. The poems that are covered in this chapter explore a range of different kinds of relationship: the father/son relationship, the mother/daughter relationship and the relationship between lovers. Some of the relationships are presented in a positive light, emphasising the feelings of happiness and security that can arise and some are presented in a negative light, emphasising feelings of anxiety and despair. At the beginning of the activities for each poem, the theme of relationships is reinforced and students are encouraged to think about why each particular poem appears in this cluster and what it has to offer in an exploration of this theme.

Throughout the chapter, students are reminded that they should always consider the theme of this cluster and think about what the individual poets are saying about relationships in each of the poems. The activities, therefore, continually link back to this theme while exploring different aspects of analysis.

 Activity This introductory activity is intended to help students connect and engage with the theme of this cluster by asking them to think about a relationship in their own life that means a lot to them. They are asked to write down what they enjoy about it and to share these thoughts with a partner. They are then asked to think about a different close relationship and to examine how this differs from the first relationship they have thought about. Many students may choose to discuss their feelings for a boyfriend/girlfriend initially so the second part of this activity is intended to widen their scope and encourage them to think about other types of relationship. This form of activity should help students to identify with the content of the following poems, which will in turn encourage a personal response to them.

Working through the chapter

Background information is given for each of the six poems in this chapter. Some biographical information is given about each poet and some introductory information about each poem is provided so that students can contextualise poems before embarking on a full analysis.

Of course, you may not have time in the classroom to explore each of the poems in the cluster in as much detail as is explored in the Student Book. The material that is presented here is intended as a suggested 'ideal' model of approach but you may only be able to select certain areas to focus on. It is hoped that you will be able to apply some, if not all, of this approach. However, it is by no means prescriptive and should not be interpreted as the number of activities that students will 'need' to have completed in preparation for their exam.

The personal response activities are crucial but by their nature are problematic to assess. For these activities, some guidance regarding the sort of response students are likely to submit is given, but this by no means should be taken as 'correct. Students should be encouraged to engage with the poems on a personal level and to feel confident in voicing their interpretations as long as they can be supported with evidence from the poem text.

Before the poems are looked at in detail, students could be reminded of the guidance on how to read a poem, guidance they first met in the Section A introduction. This summarises all the key areas that they should pay attention to as they read the Anthology poems for the first time.

'Nettles' by Vernon Scannell

Analysis activity: Exploring 'Nettles' by Vernon Scannell

This poem is suitable for students entered for both Foundation and Higher Tiers. It presents the relationship between father and son as Scannell describes his desire to protect his son from the pain caused by the stinging nettles. Another poem by Scannell, 'Growing Pains', also deals with the theme of a father's love for his son and may be further reading if students particularly like 'Nettles'.

Meaning

 Activity 1 This activity requires a personal response from students by asking them to think about an occasion from their own childhoods when they or their sibling was hurt and how their parents responded.

This introductory activity is intended to help students to identify with the content of the poem and to think about a parent's reaction.

Activity 2 This activity helps students to get to grips with the content of the poem.

Some facts that students may identify are:

- Scannell's son fell in nettles
- his son cried
- white blisters appeared on his son's skin
- Scannell slashed the nettles down and then burnt them
- the nettles grew back.

Activity 3 This activity is intended to help students identify details from the text which illustrate the poet's feelings and intentions in writing the poem.

Phrases such as 'regiment of spite', 'slashed in fury' and 'fierce parade' show the poet's anger towards the nettles. He feels bitter that they have injured his son.

Activity 4 This activity introduces students to symbolism and encourages them to think about how poets can use objects to represent the ideas and themes they wish to explore.

The nettles become a symbol for anything unpleasant that his son may have to overcome. Scannell realises that he cannot always protect his son. Sometimes, his son will have to experience bad things for himself and learn from them to help him develop as a person.

Language and imagery

Activity 5 This activity asks students to look closely at the language Scannell has used.

a Some examples of words associated with the military are: 'spears', 'regiment', 'parade', 'fallen dead', 'recruits', 'wounds'.

b Scannell uses the military metaphor for the nettles to portray the violence. He describes them as 'spears' to emphasise the damage/ injuries they can cause but he also compares them to soldiers to show they grew tall and proud. They work together like a regiment but can also fall like soldiers at war. They are not immortal. The metaphors of violence emphasise Scannell's concern for his son's wellbeing.

c The last example is the best comment as it provides both evidence and explanation of the evidence.

Activity 6 This activity asks students to examine Scannell's use of alliteration.

The alliteration is effective as it highlights the bubble shape of the blisters. We can imagine them more clearly. An example of a comment could be: 'Scannell uses alliteration to describe his son's injuries; 'white blisters beaded'. This is effective as the alliteration helps the reader to imagine the bubble shape that the blisters formed on the boy.'

Activity 7 This activity asks students to think about the poem's tone.

The rank order part of the question is a matter of opinion and should generate debate among students. The tone is quite bitter at the start with phrases such as 'regiment of spite' to describe the nettles. It changes to a tone of satisfaction as the father chops down the nettles and burns them. However, the tone becomes one of resignation at the end as he realises that the nettles have grown back and that he cannot always protect his son. Discuss with the class whether the descriptions of the tone students have selected are to be expected in a poem exploring the relationship between father and son.

Activity 8 This activity focuses student's attention on one particular line in the poem.

Scannell makes the point that 'bed' is a curious name for the nettles as we associate beds with rest, security and comfort but the nettles, in contrast, are painful and uncomfortable if you land in them.

Structure and form

Activity 9 This activity asks students to look at the rhyme scheme of the poem.

The rhyme scheme is very structured: abab, cdcd, efef, ghgh. This reinforces the continual and steady nature of the father's love for his son. The regimented and orderly rhyme scheme also highlights the military imagery in this poem.

Activity 10 This activity asks students to look at the poem's structure.

The poem has perhaps been organised into one stanza as it is about a single event and one realisation.

Activity 11 This activity draws students' attention to the punctuation in this poem.

The punctuation helps to create pauses to separate ideas. For example, the colon on the penultimate line creates a pause before the poet reveals his revelation.

Personal response

Activity 12 This activity asks students to imagine that they are the poet recounting the events in an informal letter. The task will allow them to elaborate on some facts and description but it will also provide them with an opportunity to show if they have understood the main ideas and tone of the poem.

Stretch yourself This activity can be undertaken by the higher ability students in the class. It will involve them taking a broader view and considering the subject matter of Scannell's poem and the tone he adopts to explore it. Students may wish to carry out some further reading of Scannell's poetry and perhaps that of Housman.

'Praise Song for my Mother' by Grace Nichols

This poem is suitable for students entered for both Foundation and Higher Tiers. It presents a daughter's wonder and admiration for her mother. Nichols wrote this poem as a tribute to her mother after her death.

Meaning

Activity 1 This introductory activity is intended to encourage students to think about three of the key elements in Nichols's poem: water, the moon and the sunrise.

Providing adjectives will start students considering descriptive language and imagery, which are very clear and focused in this poem.

Activity 2 This activity focuses students' attention on the references to the natural world.

Nichols has drawn upon the natural world as these are powerful elements that combine to keep the world surviving. Equally, her relationship with her mother was powerful. She presents her mother as strong, generous and nurturing. You could here instigate a discussion about the concept of Mother Nature and how this has informed Nichols's poem.

Activity 3 This activity draws students' attention to the narrative voice of the poem.

Nichols uses the personal pronouns 'you' and 'me' as it is a very personal poem about her mother and what their relationship meant to her.

Activity 4 This activity is intended to help students think about the tense a poem is written in.

The past tense indicates that the mother has died and this gives the poem a heightened level of poignancy. People often talk more fondly or reveal their true feelings for someone upon their death.

Language and imagery

Activity 5 This activity asks students to consider Nichols's use of metaphor.

One example of a metaphor is when Nichols states that her mother was 'the crab's leg/the fried plantain smell'. This reference creates wonderful images of Caribbean cooking which appeal to sight and smell. Perhaps her mother cooked these dishes or Nichols remembers her mother eating them. It could also be that these are fond memories of some of Nichols's favourite foods so she used them to show how special her mother was. This has a comforting effect on the reader, generating images of domestic bliss and a happy childhood. Encourage students to explain the effect of the metaphor they have selected.

Activity 6 This activity focuses students' attention on Nichols's use of repetition.

The repetition of 'replenishing' highlights the nurturing role that mothers provide. The metaphors that Nichols uses provide food, warmth, light and water.

Structure and form

Activity 7 This activity asks students to think about the structure of the stanzas.

The first three stanzas all state that Nichols's mother was as vital for survival as water (which is powerful) or sun (which provides warmth). The moon is perhaps included for its light and beauty. The fourth stanza lists four things as the poem gathers pace. Nichols wants to show that her mother meant many different things. Finally, the last line stands alone as it is significant and suggests that her mother nurtured her and then told her to follow her future and her dreams.

Activity 8 This activity directs students to the poem's last line.

The last line is shown to have significance by being separate from the rest of the poem. Nichols is showing that her mother provided for and nurtured her so that she could go to her 'wide futures' and be independent and successful.

Students are reminded here that they learned about the significance of the last lines in poems in Chapter 4.

Activity 9 This activity asks students to consider the rhyme-scheme of the poem.

The rhyme-scheme lends the poem a song-like quality, which is reflected in the poem's title. It could be suggested that in giving her poem this quality, Nichols is celebrating her joyous love for her mother.

Personal response

Activity 10 This activity is intended to focus students' thinking on the poet's emotions and to encourage the search for evidence to support these points.

To some extent this requires a personal response but key points are that: Nichols was clearly devoted to her mother and appreciated the way she nurtured and cared for her, and that her mother was extremely important to her, particularly while she was growing up and preparing to be independent.

Activity 11 This activity requires a personal response as it provides students with an opportunity to review what they have learned with a partner.

Stretch yourself This activity enables pupils to think about someone special to them and see if they can mirror Nichols's poem. The task pays particular attention to the structure of the poem. Encourage students to share their responses with a partner.

'How Do I Love Thee?' by Elizabeth Barrett Browning

This poem is suitable for students entered for both Foundation and Higher Tiers. It explores romantic love by joyously listing the multiple ways that the poet loves her partner.

Meaning

Activity 1 This activity is intended to help students get to grips with the content of the poem and work through some potentially unfamiliar language. Although students may first read this individually, try to ensure it is also read as a class/to the class, capturing the mood and intensity of the love within.

a Students should arrive at an answer of eight examples. These can easily be traced as you read through the poem – perhaps get the class to clap each time she presents a new example and get someone to keep tally on the board.

b The grid in the Anthology provides the first example. Check students' quotes and accompanying summaries ensuring that they are covering the 'how'. Use the responses from part (a) to aid this. These are shown in the table at the foot of the page.

This activity is replicated on Worksheet 10a in the online resources.

Activity 2 This activity asks students to focus on a particular detail of the text.

Allow the students time to explore this quote. You need to be drawing out basic needs such as air, water, food and shelter – perhaps even friendship and love. A point of debate with your class might centre around the following: is Barrett Browning referring to:

Number	Line ref	Quote	Summary of 'how' she loves her beloved
1	2–4	'... to the depth ... ideal Grace'	This is a 'spatial' metaphor in that she is almost saying, 'I love you this much.' She is describing how far, in height, width, etc. her love fills her soul. It fills further than she can see and touch. The measurements are not only physical, but spiritual.
2	5–6	'... to the level of everyday's most quiet need'	This is highlighting how her love is not just reserved for passionate and dramatic moments; it permeates her entire life and is present in the most ordinary of moments both 'by sun and candle-light'. See also Activity 2 below for discussion points here.
3	7	'... freely, as men strive for Right'	Her love is not restricted in any way and is bold like men pursuing a life of justice and honour.
4	8	'... purely, as they turn from Praise'	Her love is pure and untainted like religious belief.
5	9–10	'... with a passion put to use in my old griefs ... childhood's faith'	She is drawing on the passion previously dedicated to old worries and concerns and on the joyous, innocent faith of her childhood to love him. All of her previous emotional experiences have culminated in her current love for him.
6	11–12	'... with a love I seemed to lose ... lost saints'	Again, she refers to religious imagery and claims that her lover has re-ignited a love she felt she had lost.
7	12–13	'... with the breath ... all my life!'	The love she feels encompasses all of her being, the breath she needs to live, her happiness and her sorrow. The exclamation here emphasises her joy.
8	14	'... better after death'	She insists that she will still love her beloved after her death in the afterlife – her love will endure and remain after they have been physically parted.

- her love for her husband which is likened to one of life's basic needs to live and survive? She is not being overly dramatic, but powerful in her basic explanation that without him, she could not survive, or
- her love, from dawn to dusk, that will provide his every need? Even the simplest ('quiet') need, she will ensure he has.

Language and imagery

Activity 3 This activity asks students to look at the use of alliteration and assonance in the poem.

One example has been provided. A possible effect of this example might be that the alliteration emphasises the peace of the 'love' – the image is of still and calm, it is a love that is not forced or coerced. The teacher should go round the classroom, during this activity, and check that students are providing accurate examples of assonance and alliteration. If some students are struggling with this, perhaps choose one particularly good pairing of students to 'model' the game, illustrating good examples from the poem.

Activity 4 This activity focuses students' attention on a particular quote from the poem.

Perhaps write this quote on the board or show visual images of candlelight and sunlight as a backdrop to the discussion. You are endeavouring to draw out that 'by sun and candlelight' refers to the length of the day – from dawn until dusk/from day until night. The sentiment further enhances her expression of love. At all times of the day she will love him, meet his needs and be there for him.

Structure and form

Activity 5 This activity introduces students to the sonnet form. This sonnet adopts the Italian Petrarchan form. It employs the rhyme-scheme, abbaabba cdcdcd. The internal rhyme, along with the rhymes at the ends of the lines, helps to pull the poem together, tightly. It links the tone, meaning and emotion. Examples include, 'depth/breadth' and 'feeling' and 'ideal'.

Ask students to carry out some further research on this form so that students can effectively answer how sonnets communicate the theme of love and relationships powerfully. Some starter points are given in the Student Book.

Activity 6 This activity asks students to look at Barrett Browning's use of enjambement.

Encourage discussion here; revisit the term enjambement if necessary to ensure students are familiar with its function. Students' responses might highlight the following points:

- It is a representation of her ongoing love.
- It emphasises the measure to which her love extends.
- It shows her natural flow of love is above and beyond what might be the norm; the extended flow builds on and intensifies the love she proclaims.

Students are reminded that they learned about enjambement and its effect in Chapter 5.

Activity 7 This activity asks students to think carefully about the ending of this sonnet.

Students should be encouraged to discuss this final line with a partner or in groups and to back up the points they make with evidence from the poem.

Stretch yourself This activity introduces higher ability students to a new literary term: anaphoric.

'I love thee' is repeated ten times, if we include the title. This is constant throughout the poem – much like her love. Each time it is read, the intensity of it heightens and it contributes to the powerful and emotional force of the poem.

Students need to conclude that this repeated phrase is anaphoric, which means it is a phrase, or pronoun, that points backwards to something mentioned earlier in the text/poem. In this example, Browning is referring back to the self-posed question, 'How do I love thee?' Each repeated phrase, 'I love thee' is a point of answer. (Cataphoric is where a phrase or pronoun points forward to something mentioned later in the text/poem.)

Personal response

Activity 8 This activity asks students to write a poem following the guidelines given. The Student Book suggests creating a class display around the task.

'To His Coy Mistress' by Andrew Marvell

This poem is suitable for students entered for both Foundation and Higher Tiers. It presents the persona persuading a young lady to seize the moment and indulge in sexual gratification.

Meaning

Activity 1 This activity is designed to familiarise students with the powers and limitations of persuasion – of desiring something and endeavouring to get it – as the persona is with his mistress. Students will not only realise how words need to be specifically chosen but also how they need to be delivered to achieve a desired outcome.

Activity 2 This activity requires the students to close read the first stanza, logging all the things the persona would do to show his love if they had time on their side.

Answers will cover all examples from walking by the Indian Ganges where she belongs, presenting her with precious rubies, to the persona converting every Jew in the world for her. Students should touch on his desire to impress here also: he endeavours to impress through both his geographical as well as his biblical knowledge.

Activity 3 This activity asks students to work through the poem stanza by stanza. The following table provides some general starting responses to this.

	Summary of each stanza
Stanza 1	First stage of argument: the 'ideal'/to impress and flatter her/to seduce her with 'what ifs'/ discourse marker 'HAD time …'
Stanza 2	Second stage of argument: the 'problem'/to shock/offers the conflict with the discourse marker 'BUT'.
Stanza 3	Final stage of argument: 'the solution'/offers a remedy to the problem he delivers/discourse marker 'NOW therefore'.

One avenue of investigation here might also be to direct the students to the term *Carpe diem* – a term often levelled at this poem.

This activity is replicated on Worksheet 10b in the online resources.

Stretch yourself This activity not only encourages students to consider the formality of an argument – if it is to be convincing – but also the social, religious and cultural backdrop to this poem. Take some time to establish the expectations upon courtship in the 17th century, perhaps allocating time to research this. What expectations were placed upon the women and why? Was this expectation levelled at women of all classes? Perhaps also consider how things have changed in today's society. Is this a good thing?

Language and imagery

Activity 4 This activity asks students to look at the effect of Marvell's use of alliteration.

Building on students' analysis of the three sections to the persona's argument in **Activity 3** , students should now be aware that the first section focuses on the persona's need to impress, flatter and seduce. Hence, the rich alliteration makes this section more playful and flirty, which directly contrasts with the lack of alliteration in the next two sections which are far more serious and dismal.

The playful alliteration helps to focus the mistress's attention on certain words and levels of seduction and sentiment. The flourish of alliteration in the final couplet helps to leave his argument on an emotional high: one that is upbeat, positive and ultimately persuasive. It is the final joyous fanfare of argument to win over his intended lover.

Activity 5 This activity draws students' attention to imagery of death in the poem.

Examples from the poem that refer to death and their own mortality include:

- 'time's winged chariot'
- 'in thy marble vault'
- 'worms shall try …'
- 'turn to dust'
- '… and into ashes …'
- 'the grave's a fine and private place …'

The poet is trying to express the belief that they do not have time to wait – that 'time waits for no man'. He is impressing upon her that if they did have time on their side, then her coyness would be acceptable, but the references imply an urgency to live life for the 'now', and not defer. He is also quite serious about this; he is reminding her that mortality is no joke.

Activity 6 This activity asks students to look at the central metaphor in the poem and builds on the previous activity.

Encourage students to spend some time examining this metaphor in detail: what images initially spring to mind? Next, direct them to the link with Roman mythology and Apollo's flying chariot driving the sun. This central metaphor is the root to the persona's argument – that time does indeed 'fly' and that they have no power to stop it or slow it down. The reader can actually picture 'time' nipping at their heels; they must act now, as they do not have the luxury to be coy and wait.

Structure and form

Activity 7 This activity explores the pace of the poem.

Encourage the students to read the poem aloud. Do they notice any moments where the pace of the poem seems particularly calm, careful or indeed, fast and swifter? Investigate examples, including the following:

- Slower pace: the opening lines. Look at how the commas help to slow the pace down, ensuring the persona begins his argument in what appears a considered and rational stance.

- Quicker pace: line 41 onward. Here we see how the lack of punctuation and build up of one-syllable words intensifies the pace. It is hard to read/say, with words almost tripping over one another. The speed mirrors the persona's urgency and intensified emotion.

Students are reminded that they looked at changes of pace in Chapter 4.

Personal response

Activity 8 This activity is intended to increase the depth of analysis and autonomy over this poem. Students should not only justify and defend their point of view, but they should also use specific exemplification to platform their view.

'The Manhunt' by Simon Armitage

This poem is suitable for students entered for both Foundation and Higher Tiers. It presents the wife of an injured soldier attempting to reconnect with her physically and emotionally scarred husband.

Meaning

Activity 1 This activity is intended to make students think carefully about the title of the poem. Hold a general class discussion before reading the poem.

Activity 2 This activity asks students to think about what constitutes both war and love poetry.

Students are asked to develop a grid with words, phrases and images that might be found in both love and war poems. The grid, which has been started for the students, allows them to explore how war poems (which clearly make a comment about war and its effects) can also be the basis of a tender love poem. It encourages students to look beyond first impressions.

The previous part of this activity will have consolidated students' interpretation of the poem, 'The Manhunt'. There are several approaches to this task. Initially, students could work in pairs, discussing the three statements. Alternatively, or as an extension, you could orchestrate a class debate by dividing the class into three equal groups, allocating one statement of argument to each third. Choose a student to chair, and let the class argue their allotted point of view. Encourage them to use exemplification from the poem. Students should use this exercise as an opportunity to explore the poem's content and message, strengthening their own understanding.

This activity is replicated on Worksheet 10c in the online resources.

Activity 3 For this activity, initially allow students time to explore and consider the poet's portrayal of this painful process of recovery; students should try to imagine what the process might be like. A possible route into this could be to hot seat this from both characters' point of view, i.e. Eddie and Laura. References from the poem, that students may eventually arrive at, include:

- repetition of the 'only then' – emphasises the staged development
- progression in the poem of 'trace', to 'explore', to 'handle', to 'bind', etc.

Language and imagery

Activity 4 This activity nurtures close reading by asking students to examine the language used in the poem.

There are numerous examples of vocabulary that make one think of war and battles. Ask students to come to the front of the class and log them on the board, or, alternatively, show the poem in full on the whiteboard and ask students to come to the front and text mark. The task further asks them to ascertain what they feel is the significance of this ongoing comparison. As well as making the obvious comments on war, this poem is also making reference to the 'battle' of recovery for many of the soldiers, post war. The battle is not only personally a physical and mental one, but it becomes a battle in and around the relationships they hold.

Students are reminded that they examined extended metaphor in Chapter 3.

Activity 5 This activity has been touched on in previous tasks. As well as examples already referred to in previous activities, students may draw attention to some of the following:

- The 'delicate' process is alluded to with modifiers – 'porcelain collar bone', 'parachute silk' and 'frozen river'.
- The delicate handling of the soldier/situation/process is touched on with the symbolic reference to the 'unexploded mine'.

Try to strengthen this activity by locating some images of pinball machines on the web via video footage for them to actually visualise the speed and force with which the pinball makes its path around the machine. For this activity students must closely examine both the structure and diction of this poem. The middle section of the poem appears to spotlight the journey of the bullet 'pinballing' through Eddie's body: with every mention of 'and' (repetition) reflecting the hit and change of direction the bullet takes. Looking closely at the poem, students may note the slowing down of the pinball/bullet as it appears to 'skirt' before finally coming to rest 'beneath his chest'. Ask students to discuss the significance of the fact that this section lies at the centre of the poem.

Activity 6 This activity allows students the opportunity to explore a striking metaphor in the poem.

Students may touch on a variety of interpretations. One such interpretation might be that the disturbing image captures the horror and consequences of war. The direct reference to 'foetus' implies something that will grow or has yet to grow. Is this the injury and its impact, physically, psychologically and literally? Is the injury, and its effect, to take on a life of its own? Encourage the students to express themselves in full sentences, using direct reference to the poem. There is also irony here: a loving couple would normally be nursing the development of their foetus, instead, the couple are tending and nursing an injury from war.

Structure and form

Activity 7 This activity asks students to comment on the form and structure of the poem.

Some suggestions might cover the point that the couplets allude to the pairing of Eddie and Laura – their relationship. The full and half rhyme further signify that sometimes the battle is successful and they work together in harmony, whereas at other times, the effects of war disrupt this harmony and unison. Take valid answers from the students, encouraging explanation of their point of view.

Activity 8 This activity asks students to look closely at a particular line.

Take a range of valid answers for this statement. Students may touch on a variety of explanations ranging from the point that she came close to 'understanding' or feeling his pain. It may even allude to the fact that she came close to him letting her in, emotionally, or close to where they once were as a couple. Allow the students to debate this and, by doing so, consolidate their own interpretation.

Activity 9 This activity requires a personal response from the students – but direct them to the quote, 'a sweating, unexploded mine'. This should encourage students to explore the implications that war has on the soldiers emotionally and psychologically.

Personal response

Activity 10 This activity requires a personal response by the students. Ensure that they back up their points with evidence from the text.

Students are reminded that they looked at emotive language in Chapter 3.

'Quickdraw' by Carol Ann Duffy

This poem is suitable for students entered for both Foundation and Higher Tiers. It presents a relationship in the process of breaking down.

Meaning

Activities 1 and 2 These activities both encourage the students to conduct a first-level approach and analysis of 'Quickdraw' visually.

For Activity 2, you could, as a class, share students' work and in turn, agree on one, whole-class version that can be displayed throughout the duration of your deeper deconstruction and exploration of the poem.

This activity is replicated on Worksheet 10d in the online resources.

Activity 3 This activity asks students to think about the ambiguous narrative voice in the poem.

This activity further requires a personal point of view. It may be interesting to look at stereotypes and gender/age expectations as part of the debate. The fact that this is not gender specific could widen audience appeal and identification.

Activity 4 Students should be given time to examine this activity in pairs or groups. The extended metaphor surrounding the mobile phone gives the poem a modern context. Duffy is clearly suggesting that the phone has become quite central to how we conduct love affairs/relationships: a modern, but not necessarily positive phenomenon. Students may be able to relate to the persona's anxiety as a result of this form of communication.

Language and imagery

Activity 5 This activity asks students to highlight words and phrases which are associated with the idea of a scene from a typical Western.

There are many for the students to spot, including: 'wear ... like guns', 'slung ... hips', 'quickdraw', 'wounded', 'pellet' and 'squeeze the trigger'. Take valid explorations of this extended metaphor. Students may believe Duffy is highlighting the point that often, being in a relationship/love affair is like participating in a battle/fight of sorts: power struggles, need for control, one-upmanship, emotional struggles and combat, clashing emotionally, etc.

Activity 6 In this activity, students are directed towards the verbs, 'twirl', 'reel' and 'fumble'.

These are visual images where the persona appears to lack control, assurance, dignity and stability. Discuss with students why this might be.

Activity 7 This activity requires a personal written response from each student.

Depending on the ability of the students, get lower ability students to pair up with stronger students initially to discuss this task, before moving on to independent writing. Share examples as a class to strengthen understanding through peer observation.

Activity 8 This activity requires students to examine Duffy's use of alliteration.

The example highlighted sounds clumsy to say; the 'f'/'f'/'f' sounds almost stumbling over each other, further reinforcing the lack of control the persona has over this situation and his/her feelings. There is a sense of indignity here.

Activity 9 This activity asks students to consider the tone of the poem.

This activity could be conducted as a card-sorting exercise, encouraging the students to rank order the descriptions which, for them, best describe the tone of the poem. This rank ordering could then be shared with the class, discussing the most to least appropriate. A league table displaying most appropriate tone could be put on view while this poem is being analysed further.

Structure and form

Activity 10 This activity asks students to comment on the structure of the poem, drawing on previous study around sonnets – with a particular slant on the English sonnet.

Students may highlight that it has loose associations with the sonnet, reinforcing the theme of love, but likewise reinforcing that the lack of strict metre or rhyme alludes to the lack of order and stability to this love affair; it is a diluted version of what it once was/could have been.

Activity 11 This activity asks students to look at the positioning of words in the poem.

Ask students to copy this statement out onto a strip of paper, then, cut it in half through the words 'me' and 'through'. Does it symbolise the broken heart? Is the split the damage of the 'bullet' tearing them apart? Take appropriate responses as to why this line sits at the heart of the poem in light of previous discussions.

Students are reminded that they looked at the positioning of words in Chapter 5.

Activity 12 This activity will allow the students to strengthen their interpretation and understanding of the poem by examining two words in context of the poem as a whole and the associated themes and messages.

Get the students to observe who/what/how/why around each word, perhaps as a spider diagram. Take feedback and encourage explanation and discussion.

Personal response

Activity 13 This activity asks students to consider whether the poem makes them feel anxious. Students may well be able to relate to the feeling of angst present in the poem and so some interesting discussion could be generated.

Comparing poems in the 'Relationships' cluster

Planning activity: Comparing Rossetti and Mew

At the end of this chapter, students are provided with some guidance as to how to approach the comparison element of the Anthology examination question (Unit 2A). In the exam, students will be asked to analyse a set poem from the 'Relationships' cluster; this could be any poem from the cluster so it is important that students are prepared to respond confidently to all of the poems in this cluster. Students will also be asked to analyse one other poem of their choice from the cluster in light of the focus of the question. For example, students may be asked:

> Compare how the parent/child relationship is presented in 'Nettles' and one other poem from the 'Relationships' cluster. *(36 marks)*

Analysing the question

It is of vital importance that students understand what is being asked of them in the exam. A sample question is annotated in the Student Book with the five key elements that students are required to address:

1 A **comparison** must be made
2 The poet's **techniques** must be examined
3 The **focus area** must be clear in student's minds
4 The **named poem** must be covered in the student's response
5 **One other** poem must be included in the analysis.

Activity 1 This activity asks students to annotate further sample questions in the same way to consolidate their learning.

Choosing your comparison poem

Remind students that the choice they make regarding the second poem they are to analyse is crucial. They need to select a poem that will provide them with enough material to enable them to make a full and effective comparison, both in terms of the similarities between the poems and also the differences between them. Students should be able to compare:

- the attitudes and ideas presented
- the language and imagery used
- the structure and form of the poems.

Students have been working through the poems presented in this chapter according to these areas of analysis. The chapters of Section A, where these different aspects are individually introduced and explored, will provide further assurance for students wishing to revise the sort of techniques and devices they should be looking out for.

In planning their response, students are encouraged to record their initial ideas in a grid. This will help to direct their thoughts and discourage them from straying from the focus of the question. It will also enable them to clearly see the points of similarity and of difference between the two poems. The grid provided uses 'How Do I Love Thee?' as an example.

Activity 2 This activity asks students to complete their own grid using an alternative comparison poem of their choice. This should illustrate to students that a variety of poems can be chosen for comparison – but that some choices are more effective than others.

This activity is replicated on Worksheet 10e in the online resources.

Structuring your answer

Once students are clear about what they need to do and the points they wish to cover, they can think about their opening paragraph. Encourage students to use this paragraph both for their own reference, to outline what they intend to cover in their essay and to ensure that they are clearly establishing the focus of their response for the examiner. This paragraph should immediately demonstrate skills of comparison. A sample paragraph is provided.

Activity 3 This activity asks students to write their own opening paragraph for their chosen comparison.

Students are then advised to draw on discourse markers to illustrate points of comparison in the main section of their response.

It is worth reinforcing at this stage that students should remember to consider the differences and contrasts between poems in addition to examining the similarities between them.

Activity 4 This activity asks students to write a paragraph in which they develop their comparison with the poem of their choice and underline the words that indicate that a comparison is being made. This should reinforce with students the need to constantly compare one poem with another.

Reinforce with students the need to explain **how** and **why** a poet is creating certain effects rather than simply recounting which devices a poet has used. Also encourage students to make a personal response – examiners will be looking for evidence of engagement with the text.

Students are finally advised to make an insightful comment in their closing paragraph to illustrate that they are comparing the poems to the end of their essay.

Activity 5 This activity asks students to write their final paragraph and to include their final pertinent point.

Students could contribute alternative questions to help them to become comfortable with the structure of the question. This would encourage them to think about potential pairings of poems in readiness for the exam.

Remind students to bear in mind the theme of 'Relationships' throughout their analysis. What do the poems they are writing about offer in an exploration of this theme?

Outcomes

Interactive activity: Examining the form of some of the poems in the 'Relationships' cluster

In this chapter students have learned how to:

- approach analysing poems in the 'Relationships' cluster
- compare two poems in the exam.

11 Making your skills count in the exam: the Anthology question

AO focus

AO1: Respond to texts critically and imaginatively; select and evaluate relevant textual detail to illustrate and support interpretation.

AO2: Explain how language, structure and form contribute to writers' presentation of ideas, themes and settings.

AO3: Make comparisons and explain links between texts, evaluating writers' different ways of expressing meaning and achieving effects.

In this chapter your students will:

- learn about what is required of them in the exam for Unit 2, Section A: Poetry Across Time
- apply and practise their skills in order to respond to the exam question effectively.

About the exam

Structure and content of the exam

Unit 2, Section A: Poetry Across Time will be based on the poetry in the Anthology. The Unit covers two poetry eras: contemporary poetry and poetry from the English, Welsh and Irish, Literary Heritage. The poems are arranged into four thematic clusters:

- Characters and voices
- Place
- Conflict
- Relationships

Each cluster contains 15 poems and covers the two poetry eras. Candidates must study one cluster and answer a question on this cluster in the exam. There will be a choice of two questions for each cluster on the exam paper and students must answer one of these relating to the cluster they have studied. The questions ask students to compare a named poem from the cluster with another poem of their choice, also from the same cluster, and with a specific focus. The questions are worth 36 marks, 23 per cent of their total GCSE mark; candidates are advised to spend 45 minutes on this part of the paper.

In this Unit, candidates will take a skills-based approach to poetry in order to become engaged and critical readers. This means that they will be expected to respond to:

- ideas, themes and issues
- language (including sound and imagery), form and structure.

They will be expected to make comparisons across poems in the cluster they have studied. Through their study, they will learn how to make informed, personal responses to poetry and to offer an interpretation of a poem which can be supported by textual evidence.

How to prepare candidates for the exam

Planning activity: Characters and voices

Candidates will have read all the poems in one of the clusters. They will need to be confident about knowing the meanings of the more obscure words in these poems. It would be useful to teach some of the linguistic terms which can be used to analyse poetry.

Useful terms for comparison include:

- in a similar way
- both poets
- compared to
- however
- unlike
- in contrast to
- whereas
- on the other hand

Teachers should consider the best poems to compare and practise some sample comparisons. It is important to choose the second poem wisely. Not all the poems link effectively; some are too different from each other, so candidates will need to have in mind, well before the exam, which poems work successfully together. The second poem must have enough in common with the first as well as enough significant differences. If the poems have little in common the comparative essay will be difficult to write.

Remember these key points the examiners will be looking for:

Relevance: Candidates will need to read the question carefully and show how the two poems (one of which they will choose) link together, looking for contrasts and comparisons.

Personal response: The examiners are looking for a personal reaction to the two poems (there is no 'correct' answer).

Analysis: Candidates should show that they have engaged with the text and can provide detail to support their interpretations.

Exploration: Candidates should be able to offer an insightful response to the text and infer their own conclusions from it.

Communication: Candidates must make sure they communicate their ideas clearly and accurately.

What students need to know

Candidates should:

- read the question carefully
- underline the key words in the question, to help focus on answering it successfully
- follow any bullet points in the question
- make a plan
- integrate short quotations into their writing
- be aware of time: they have 45 minutes for this question and should spend an equal amount of time on each part
- allow themselves time to check their answers for sense and for any errors of spelling and punctuation.

Introducing the questions

In the Student Book and in the online resources there are some sample questions and answers to typical exam-type questions.

The questions below are typical of the ones that will be in the examination. These questions are based on the poems 'The Wild Swans at Coole' by W B Yeats and 'Cold Knap Lake' by Gillian Clarke, from the 'Place' cluster.

Foundation Tier

The question would be structured as follows for Foundation students:

> 1 Compare how the poets present place in 'The Wild Swans at Coole' and **one** other poem from the 'Place' in your Anthology.
>
>   Remember to compare:
>   - the places in the poems
>   - how the places are presented.
>
>   *(36 marks)*

Examiners will be looking for evidence that students have explored the **content** of the poems (*what* the poet is presenting), the **techniques** that the poets have used (*how* the poet presents the

content) and how the poems can be **compared and contrasted**.

Content

For mid-range marks candidates should demonstrate:

- **sustained** response to elements of the text
- effective use of details to support their interpretation
- thoughtful consideration of ideas/themes with detail.

For high marks candidates should demonstrate:

- **considered/qualified** response to the text
- details linked to interpretation (the answer should not just be what the poem is about, or what it describes, but also what the poet's ideas, thoughts and attitudes are).
- appropriate comment on ideas/themes.

Techniques

Candidates should focus on use of **language** and/or **structure** and/or **form** and their **effects** on readers.

For mid-range marks candidates should demonstrate:

- **explanation** of effect(s) of writer's uses of language and/or structure and/or form and effects on readers.

For high marks candidates should demonstrate:

- an **appreciation/consideration** of writers' uses of language and/or structure and/or form and effects on readers.

Candidates should be reminded that it is not just a matter of naming features, such as metaphor, but they should also explain their *purpose* and *effects*. (Use the PEE method: Point, Example, Explain.)

Comparison

For comments please see Higher Tier guidance.

Higher tier

An example of a Higher Tier question would be:

> 1 Compare how Yeats presents the effects of nature on man in 'The Wild Swans at Coole' and **one** other poem from 'Place'.
>
>   *(36 marks)*

Here the guiding bullet points will not be provided. The response to this question will be expected to be more analytical and evaluative than the equivalent response at Foundation Tier.

Content and techniques

For mid-range marks candidates should be able to demonstrate:

- **considered/qualified** response to the text
- details linked to interpretation
- **appreciation/consideration** of writers' uses of language and/or structure and/or form and effects on readers
- **thoughtful** consideration of ideas/themes.

For high marks candidates should be able to demonstrate:

- **insightful exploratory** response to the texts
- **close** analysis of detail to support interpretation, e.g. several things suggested about the meaning of the swans
- **evaluation** of the writers' uses of language and/or structure and or/form and effects on readers, e.g. a discussion of the metaphors in the poem
- **convincing/imaginative** interpretation of ideas/themes, e.g. a convincing exploration of the effects of nature on the poet.

Candidates should be encouraged to work at how to show empathy; they should be able to appreciate the poet's concerns, ideas or views with a high degree of personal involvement.

Comparison

Both Foundation and Higher students should focus their response around **comparison**. Candidates should show the examiner why they have chosen their second poem. They should look at the named poem in detail and go on to look at the second poem, making comparisons with the first poem, using some of the suggested expressions given above.

Candidates will need to look out for:

- similarities in the approaches the poets have taken to the theme
- differences between the writers' approaches to there
- comparisons and contrasts in the way the poets have used language to express their ideas, for example they could consider the use and effect of repetition
- comparisons and contrasts in the way that poets have used structure and form, e.g. they could look at any rhyme in both poems

At **Foundation** Tier, for mid-range marks candidates should be able to demonstrate:

- **sustained** focus on similarities/differences in terms of ideas/themes, with detail
- **sustained** focus on similarities/differences in terms of writers' uses of language and/or structure and/or form, with detail.

For high marks candidates should be able to demonstrate:

- **developed** comparison in terms of ideas/themes, with detail
- **developed** comparison in terms of writers' uses of language and/or structure and/or form and effects on readers, with detail.

At **Higher** Tier, for mid-range marks candidates should be able to show:

- **sustained** focus on similarities/differences in terms of ideas/themes
- **sustained** focus on similarities/difference in terms of writers' uses of language and/or structure and/or form
- selection of material for a range of comparison.

For high marks candidates should be able to demonstrate:

- **evaluative** comparison of ideas/themes in the poems, with detail, e.g. a comparison of how the lake is used as a theme in both poems
- **evaluative** comparison of the poets' uses of language and/or structure and/or form and the effects on readers, e.g. a comparison of the use of metaphors.

Practice exam questions

[kt] On your marks activity: 'Place'
[kt] On your marks activity: 'Conflict'

Students are provided with sample exam questions for both Higher and Foundation Tier in the Student Book.

Outcomes

In this chapter students have learned how to:

- prepare for Section A of Unit 2 of the exam
- write a comprehensive response to the question set.

AO focus

AO1: Respond to texts critically and imaginatively; select and evaluate relevant textual detail to illustrate and support interpretation.

AO2: Explain how language, structure and form contribute to writers' presentation of ideas, themes and settings.

AO3: Make comparisons and explain links between texts, evaluating writers' different ways of expressing meaning and achieving effects.

In this chapter your students will:

- learn about what is required of them for the controlled assessment for Unit 5: Exploring Poetry
- apply and practice their skills in order to complete the controlled assessment effectively.

What is controlled assessment?

The controlled assessment for Unit 5 should take up to 4 hours, is worth 40 marks and makes up 25 per cent of the total GCSE mark.

There are three elements to controlled assessment:

- Task setting
- Task taking
- Task marking

AQA's controlled assessment tasks allow you the flexibility to:

- choose texts
- contextualise tasks to meet the needs of your students
- timetable the assessment to meet your needs
- offer assessment in January and June.

The tasks will not be prescriptive, they will be purely illustrative. Centres may contextualise tasks by selecting poems which will meet the needs of their candidates. A whole poetry text is made up of 15 poems, but the final assessment can be based on a smaller number of poems. Candidates must complete one task which will be based on a comparison of poems. They will be encouraged to make creative links, choosing poems from the range studied. They must write about the poems from two periods: contemporary and English, Welsh and Irish Literary Heritage. Contemporary poetry means poetry that is being written by living poets such as Carol Ann Duffy, Seamus Heaney and Andrew

Motion. The Literary Heritage includes poets with an enduring appeal that transcends the period in which they were writing, for example the poetry of John Donne, TS Eliot and Shakespeare continue to be widely read, studied and interpreted for contemporary audiences. Students' study should be based on whole texts and can be supported by multi-modal texts. For example, candidates may consider how audio versions of the text offer new or different interpretations of the texts. This should be clearly linked to the written text and should illuminate the writers' techniques. You may wish to use poems from the AQA Anthology or you may wish to use a range of poems of your own choice.

Students will be expected to make links and draw comparisons between the poems studied. As students will have more time available to them than is the case in examination conditions, the comparisons made must be wide-ranging and fully developed.

Task setting

Tasks will be set by AQA. Each year AQA will provide a bank of tasks – one for each of the topics covered in this unit:

- themes and ideas
- aspects of genre and form.

The tasks will be published on the AQA website and you will have access to them from 1 April in the year before the year in which students are entered for the unit.

The tasks will offer a variety of approaches and may consist of simply a title or may contain further bullet points to help structure students' responses.

Topic 1: Themes and ideas

Under each heading tasks may be set on aspects such as:

- conflict
- love
- family
- power.

Topic 2: Aspects of genre and form

Planning activity: genre and form

- Endings
- Importance of parts to whole
- Setting
- Conventions

Task taking

Students will submit one task chosen from the topics in this Unit. They must produce work totalling about 2000 words in a period of up to four hours in response to the controlled assessment task. They will use clean, unannotated copies of the texts during the assessment period. While they are writing up their responses they must work completely independently and complete all work under formal supervision, by either you as their teacher, or an invigilator. They may either produce their controlled assessment in one four-hour session or in shorter sessions. They will not be able to receive any feedback. They will be allowed access to dictionaries and thesauri and to grammar and spell check programmes. They will be able to handwrite their assessment or produce it electronically.

Assessment Objectives (Task marking)

The Assessment Objectives relevant to this Unit are as follows:

AO1: Respond to texts critically and imaginatively; select and evaluate relevant textual detail to illustrate and support interpretations.

AO2: Explain how language, structure and form contribute to writers' presentation of ideas, themes and settings.

AO3: Make comparisons and explain links between texts, evaluating writers' different ways of expressing meaning and achieving effects.

Preparing for the controlled assessment

You should prepare candidates by teaching approaches to the assessment, and by studying style models which may include exemplar responses by other students. You should also ensure that candidates are familiar with the assessment criteria for the controlled assessment tasks and are aware of the weighting given to each assessment objective.

You can allocate as much time as you wish to planning, but you need to bear in mind the marks and weighting allocated to each controlled assessment (refer to the AQA spec for these).

Having taught approaches to the topics and studied relevant models for the final assessment you should give candidates the relevant task. During this time, candidates should have access to relevant source materials to inform their preparation.

Introducing the questions

Set out below are some AQA-type controlled assessment questions:

Themes and ideas
Family

Overview of the topic: Within the topic of 'Themes and ideas' a subtopic could be 'family'. Students could be asked, for example, to compare the ways family relationships are presented in the poems they have studied. They could look at parents or children and feelings towards them.

Key words and phrases might include:

- Explore the ways in which the parent/child relationship is presented...
- How does the poet present thoughts and feelings about parenthood...
- Explore ways of making the experiences, ideas and feelings clear to a listener who is using poetry readings on an MP3 player to revise for GCSE.

Aspects of genre and form
Conventions

Overview of the topic: Within the topic of 'Aspects of genre and form' a subtopic could be 'conventions'. Students will need to look at the form of the poems, for example the sonnet form, and consider how to compare poems that use the same form. They will need to consider the significance of the form to the whole text.

Key words and phrases might include:

- Explore the ways the sonnet form is used by [Shakespeare] to develop ideas.
- Compare how a contemporary poet uses the sonnet form to develop ideas.

Skills

For both of the above topic areas the following scheme is applicable.

For lower-range marks, the key words are 'clear ... consistent'. Candidates will be expected to demonstrate:

- a **clear** understanding of the writers' ideas
- the ability to use relevant and appropriate supporting textual detail
- a **clear** understanding of features of language and structure supported by relevant and appropriate quotation

- a **clear** understanding of links and some points of comparison between texts.

For mid-range marks, the key words are 'confident … assured'. Candidates will be expected to demonstrate:

- **sustained and developed** appreciation of writers' ideas and attitudes and provide convincing interpretations using precisely selected supporting detail

- **analysis** of aspects of language and structure in convincing detail

- **thoughtful consideration** of comparisons between texts.

For higher-range marks, the key words are 'sophisticated … impressive'. Candidates will be expected to demonstrate:

- **sophisticated engagement** with writers' ideas and attitudes – they develop sophisticated interpretations using imaginatively selected supporting textual detail

- **sophisticated analysis** of aspects of language and structure

- **perceptive and imaginative exploration** of points of linkage and comparison.

You as a teacher will be looking for how well students demonstrate the skills above. For grade C you will be looking for *clear and consistent* answers, for grade B you will be looking for *confident and assured* answers and for grade A, *sophisticated and impressive* answers.

How to use the time available

Preparation and planning

Students will need plenty of practice in preparing for controlled assessment. You as a teacher should give students the chance to practise writing and to prepare ideas. Students will need to keep all records of preparatory work. They will be able to work with others and discuss their ideas in a small group, but their response to the task will be as an individual. As the controlled assessment makes up 25 per cent of the total GCSE mark, you are advised to spend 25 per cent of the time available to you on the texts and the topic chosen.

AQA controlled assessment-style questions

The following is used as a sample task in the Student Book:

Themes and ideas
Conflict

Outline question:

> 1 Explore the ways conflict is presented and developed in the poems you have studied.
>
> (*40 marks*)

An example of how this could be developed:

> a) How does Tennyson present conflict in 'The Charge of the Light Brigade'?
>
> b) Compare Tennyson's poem with how two other poets present conflict.

This example question (task) is similar to the type that will be supplied by AQA. The teacher or the students themselves will choose the poems to be assessed. Teachers will be able to develop the question as they see fit. One way of developing the outline question above could be to evaluate a certain aspect of the question in part (a). The second part of the assessment (b) must be a comparison exercise. You, with your students, will have a free choice of the poems you use for comparison.

Ideas for how to respond to this task are given in the Student Book.

Two further AQA type tasks are given below, from the topics **Themes and ideas** and **Aspects of genre and form**.

Themes and ideas
Relationships

Outline question:

> 1 Explore the way the relationships between characters are presented and developed in the texts you have studied.
>
> (*40 marks*)

An example of how this could be developed:

> a) How does Dylan Thomas reveal the isolation of the main character in 'The Hunchback in the Park'?
>
> b) Compare this with how two contemporary poets reveal the isolation of their main characters. (Suitable poems would be: 'The Clown Punk' by Simon Armitage and 'Medusa' by Carol Ann Duffy.)

Aspects of genre and form

Conventions

Outline question:

1   Explore how the sonnet form is used to develop ideaas in the poems you have studied.   *(40 marks)*

An example of how this could be developed:

a   How does Shakespeare use the sonnet form to develop his ideas?   b   Compare this with how two contemporary poets use the sonnet form to develop their ideas.

Outcomes

In this chapter students have learned how to:

- prepare for the controlled assessment task for Unit 5
- write a comprehensive response to the task set.

Section C: Short stories

Introduction

The Section opener in the Student Book explains the text choice that is available to centres for Unit 1; students can study from either the set novels or the short stories from the Anthology. The short stories can be studied as one set text for Section A of Unit 1 which is titled 'Modern Prose or Drama' – this means continuous prose written after 1945. Within the *Sunlight on the Grass* short stories Anthology, there are seven short stories which have been written by authors from varying cultural backgrounds. The following three stories have been included in the Student Book:

- 'The Darkness Out There' by Penelope Lively
- 'Compass and Torch' by Elizabeth Baines
- 'Anil' by Ridjal Noor

The remaining four stories are covered in the online materials that accompany the Student Book. These are:

- 'On Seeing the 100% Perfect Girl One Beautiful April Morning' by Haruki Murakami
- 'My Polish Teacher's Tie' by Helen Dunmore
- 'When the Wasps Drowned' by Clare Wigfall
- 'Something Old, Something New' by Leila Aboulela

The key thing to remember when preparing students for the Anthology short stories is that you do not know which stories will appear on the exam paper so students must be prepared for all seven.

The modern prose question that students will answer in the exam will require them to analyse a particular aspect of one of the short stories. They will then have to analyse the same aspect in one other of the short stories – which they can choose. That is why it is important that students are taught to see the links between the short stories; although they do not need to directly compare them in the exam.

The following prompts may be useful for students when they initially read a short story:

- Pay close attention to the opening. Identify the narrative hooks that have been used.
- Look at how characters have been developed. Verbs and adjectives are often used to great effect as we have to learn about characters quickly. What do the characters say and how does their behaviour reveal something about them?
- Consider the setting – again this has to be created quickly. Look at how the senses are used.
- What are the themes? The writer has a limited amount of time in which to reveal the ideas and issues that they wish to either support or challenge.
- Think about the context – this is very important so be aware of any clues that establish the social, cultural and historical background.
- How does the ending make you feel?

Assessment Objectives

There are two Assessment Objectives for this part of the paper:

AO1: Respond to texts critically and imaginatively; select and evaluate relevant textual detail to illustrate and support interpretation.

AO2: Explain how language, structure and form contribute to writers' presentation of ideas, themes and settings.

These objectives could form a peer- or self-assessment checklist about what the students can do when studying short stories:

- I can analyse short stories by commenting on features such as: setting, point of view, character, themes and structure.
- I can identify relevant quotations to justify and support the comments I have made.
- I can identify and explain some of the ways that the writer has used language.

Approaching short stories

Here are a few generic ideas on how to approach the Anthology short stories:

- A jigsaw approach could be used to study a short story. The story could be split into sections and a different group could work on a different section. They would become experts on this bit of the story as they would comment on character, setting, language, structure, etc. The groups could then be reformed to include one person from each expert group and each person has to inform the others about their section of the story.
- You could model how to annotate a section of the story such as the opening and then ask students to apply the same skills to the ending or another section of a story.
- Students could create mind maps on the characters or themes within a story. Eventually, this could also be used to trace one theme across the set of short stories.
- Students could be set a quest to find things within a story, for example an instance of direct speech, a simile, etc. Different coloured highlighters could be used to identify different features.
- Students could match up character cards and character descriptions.
- Students could create story boards/timelines to extract the key parts of the plot.
- Students could play 'True or False?' in response to a series of questions on the plot, characters, language, etc.
- Students could match up quotations and explanations.
- Students could write summaries for each part of a story: following the pyramid plot structure.

Nelson Thornes resources

Chapter	Student Book stories and activities	(k!) resources
13. How to read short stories	**What is a short story?** 1: Analysing features of a short story **Setting** 2: Explaining what makes a successful short story **Point of view** 1–2: Analysing the use of setting in short stories 3: Exploring the use and effects of first and third person narrative in short stories **Character** 1–2: Analysing types of characters 3: Explaining how writers describe characters **Themes** 1–2: Understanding themes found in the short stories 3: Looking at the development of a theme **Structure** 1–2: Researching types of structure	Interactive activity: 'When the Wasps Drowned' Viewpoints activity: Narration in 'When the Wasps Drowned' Analysis activity: Analysing 'When the Wasps Drowned' Interactive activity: Chronology of 'My Polish Teacher's Tie' Analysis activity: 'My Polish Teacher's Tie' Analysis activity: 'Something Old, Something New' 1 Interactive activity: 'Something Old, Something New' 2 Interactive activity: 'Something Old, Something New' 3 Interactive activity: 'Something Old, Something New' Analysis activity: 'On Seeing the 100% Perfect Girl One Beautiful April Morning' Viewpoints activity: 'On Seeing the 100% Perfect Girl One Beautiful April Morning' Viewpoints activity: Do short stories have as much value as novels? Analysis activity: Setting in short stories Interactive activity: Character types Interactive activity: The short happy life of Frances Macomber Interactive activity: A man and a woman Interactive activity: Short story themes Interactive activity: Grabbing the reader's attention Interactive activity: Story endings Interactive activity: Story terms 1 Interactive activity: Story terms 2 Interactive activity: Multiple-choice quiz on short stories Worksheet 13a: Character, Activity 2 Worksheet 13b: Themes, Activity 2
14. 'The Darkness Out There'	1–3: Reflecting on the idea of 'stereotypes' **Setting** 4–8: Analysing the writer's use of setting **Point of view** 9–11: Explaining the points of view presented **Character** 12–21: Analysing the writer's presentation and use of characters	Analysis activity: Analysing 'The Darkness Out There' Interactive activity: Responding to 'The Darkness Out There'

Chapter	Student Book stories and activities	(k!) resources
14. 'The Darkness Out There' *continued*	**Themes** Stretch yourself: Writing a diary entry from Kerry's and Mrs Rutter's point of view 22–23: Analysing the development of themes in the story **Structure** 24: Explaining how the writer uses structure	Worksheet 14a: Activity 3 Worksheet 14b: Setting, Activity 6 Worksheet 14c: Character, Activity 18 Worksheet 14d: Character, Activity 19
15. 'Compass and Torch'	1–3: Reflecting on first impressions **Setting** 4–7: Analysing the writer's use of setting **Point of view** 8–11: Explaining the points of view presented **Character** 12–15: Analysing the writer's presentation and use of characters Stretch yourself: Writing a diary entry from the point of view of the boy 16–18: Further analysis of the writer's presentation and use of characters Stretch yourself: Role-playing conversations between characters and writing a letter from the point of view of the dad **Themes** 19–21: Analysing the development of themes in the story **Structure** 22–25: Explaining how the writer uses structure	Analysis activity: Analysing 'Compass and Torch' Viewpoints activity: 'Compass and Torch' Worksheet 15a: Point of view, Activity 10
16. 'Anil'	1–2: Reflecting on the cultural context **Setting** 3–6: Analysing the writer's use of setting **Point of view** 7–8: Explaining the points of view presented **Character** 9–14: Analysing the writer's presentation and use of characters Stretch yourself: Hot-seating characters **Themes** 15–17: Analysing the development of themes in the story Stretch yourself: Writing a letter from the point of view of the father 18: Further analysis of the development of themes **Structure** 19–21: Explaining how the writer uses structure	Interactive activity: 'Anil' Analysis activity: 'Anil' Worksheet 16a: Activity 2 Worksheet 16b: Character, Activity 9 Worksheet 16c: Character, Activity 14 Worksheet 16d: Structure, Activity 19
17. Making your skills count in the exam: the Short Stories question	Analysing sample example questions, student responses and examiner comments	Planning activity: 'On Seeing the 100% Perfect Girl One Beautiful April Morning' On your marks activity: 'Anil' On your marks activity: 'Something Old, Something New'

AO focus

AO1: Respond to texts critically and imaginatively; select and evaluate relevant textual detail to illustrate and support interpretation.

AO2: Explain how language, structure and form contribute to writers' presentation of ideas, themes and settings.

In this chapter your students will:

- learn about the genre of the short story
- look at how to analyse a short story's setting
- look at the point of view presented in a short story
- examine the characterisation in a short story
- consider the themes that the write of a short story may wish to raise
- analyse the common structures that a short story can have.

In this chapter, students are introduced to the short story genre and are provided with an approach to analysis. In a similar fashion to the approach taken to studying poetry earlier in the Student Book, this chapter works through different points of analysis in turn and introduces students to the key terms they will need to know to conduct a thorough and effective investigation. The chapter explores the setting, point of view, characterisation, theme and structure of short stories; outlining for each the essential points students need to learn and including activities which draw on extracts from some of the set short stories as examples. These sub-headings are then applied to three of the set short stories in the following chapters. It is hoped that this consistent and logical approach will increase students' confidence by equipping them with a clear method with which to apply their skills of analysis.

Key terms

Key terms the students are introduced to in this chapter:

- Narrative
- Context
- Symbolism
- Perspective
- Bias
- Omniscient
- Viewpoint
- Characterisation
- Implied

Short stories included in this chapter

Three of the set short stories are covered in dedicated chapters of the Student Book: the remainder are covered in the online resources.

Short stories used as examples in this introductory chapter:

- 'The Darkness Out There' by Penelope Lively
- 'My Polish Teacher's Tie' by Helen Dunmore
- 'Anil' by Ridjal Noor
- 'On Seeing the 100% Perfect Girl One Beautiful April Morning.'

These stories are covered by online resources:

- Interactive activity: 'When the Wasps Drowned' by Clare Wigfall
- Viewpoints activity: Narration in 'When the Wasps Drowned'
- Analysis activity: Analysing 'When the Wasps Drowned'
- Interactive activity: Chronology of 'My Polish Teacher's Tie'
- Interactive activity: Aspects of 'My Polish Teacher's Tie'
- Analysis activity: 'My Polish Teacher's Tie'
- Analysis activity: 'Something Old, Something New' 1
- Interactive activity: 'Something Old, Something New' 2
- Interactive activity: 'Something Old, Something New' 3
- Analysis activity: 'On Seeing the 100% Perfect Girl One Beautiful April Morning'
- Viewpoints activity: 'On Seeing the 100% Perfect Girl One Beautiful April Morning'
- Viewpoints activity: Do short stories have as much value as novels?

Additional resources

Worksheets:

- 13a: Character Activity 2
- 13b: Themes Activity 2

Getting started

What is a short story?

This chapter advises students on how to read short stories. The first part of the chapter is intended to help students to differentiate clearly between novels and short stories and to understand the opportunities and limitations of writing both forms.

Activity 1 This activity will require students to focus on some of the key differences between short stories and novels.

Encourage discussion around each of the short statements before students commit to entering them in the Venn diagram. Use the following as guidance.

Short story	Short story	Novel
Both	Both	Short story
Novel	Short story	Novel
Novel	Short story	Novel

You could use this discussion to gather and collate student's current knowledge of the short story genre. Some students may already be familiar with the genre while some may have no experience of it, so this activity provides the opportunity to ensure that all students are well positioned to move on to more detailed analysis.

Activity 2 This activity asks students to discuss what makes a short story successful.

This requires a personal response from students and they should be encouraged to make appropriate suggestions. You could facilitate student opinion by getting them to refer to/cite specific short stories they have read, detailing why they were drawn into the narrative.

Working through the chapter

Of course, you may not have time in the classroom to explore each of the set short stories in as much detail as is explored in the Student Book. The material that is presented here is intended as a suggested 'ideal' model of approach but you may only be able to select certain areas to focus on. It is hoped that you will be able to apply some, if not all, of this approach; however, it is by no means prescriptive and should not be interpreted as the number of activities that students will need to have completed in preparation for their exam.

Setting

Analysis activity: Setting in short stories

This section explores the impact of setting in short stories. Setting is defined here as the time, place and situation in which the narrative of the short story is developed. Students are introduced to the importance of the cultural background of a short story's narrative in establishing a context which

informs the progression of the plot. Students are also introduced to the symbolism of some settings and the ways that a setting can enhance and reinforce the overall intention and message of a short story.

Activity 1 This activity asks students to examine how Penelope Lively establishes setting in 'The Darkness Out There'.

For this activity students need to focus on the two extracts provided. Each extract has been annotated to start students thinking and each gives the students a route into writing their targeted comments. Some starting points might further include:

- What we learn about the setting

Extract one: The setting leading up to Mrs Rutter's house seems quintessentially rural, picturesque and appealing. It seems idyllic.

Extract two: This setting is unpleasant and run-down. There is abandoned debris and the plants and trees seem unwelcoming.

- The atmosphere created

Extract one: inviting, warm, peaceful and pleasant.

Extract two: ominous, intense, foreboding and threatening.

- The contrast presented

The contrast is quite distinct and serves to remind the reader not to be lulled into a false sense of security by instant appearances. The contrast heightens the shock of the unfolding story. We as the reader are not expecting it; the chocolate-box appearance was a façade that covers a deeper, more sinister truth.

Activity 2 This activity asks students to consider a selection of photographs in light of what they suggest about the setting of a plot.

This activity requires a personal response from the students. Ensure each student provides exemplification and justification for the responses they give. You may see a range of responses: some may go for the obvious traffic jam and the images of rain and squalor as an impetus to nurture change. However, others might use the cold, almost clinical and methodical blandness of the luxurious house as background to a need to go in pursuit of excitement.

Quick questions to ask about setting

These bullet points are intended to help students consider and explore the setting of a short story. They can be asked at the beginning of an analysis of setting in order to focus students' attention or as a revision exercise to remind students of the sorts of things to be looking out for. Students are reminded to ask:

- **where** a narrative is set
- **when** the narrative takes place
- what the **context** of the setting is.

Remind students to provide evidence from the text to support their conclusions regarding these points. You should encourage students to think about the effect of each of these points and to consider how it affects their interpretation of the short story as a whole.

Point of view

This section explains the different basic types of narration that writers can adopt to tell their story. Students are encouraged to think about whose point of view they are being presented with in a story and to consider how much they can find out objectively from this perspective.

First person narration

First person narration is defined and exemplified. Students are introduced to both the benefits of this form of narration – it can encourage a strong relationship between the character and the reader – and its drawbacks – the limitations of bias and only exploring one perspective.

Activity 1 This activity focuses students' attention on an example of first person narration from 'My Polish Teacher's Tie'.

This activity may lead to further deconstruction of the text. However, as a starting point, students should be providing responses that may touch on the following:

a Carla is a dinner lady. She appears not to like the monotony of her job and the lack of challenge and fulfilment it brings. She does appear to like the students at the school and being part of this environment. She doesn't appear to value either her work or herself. References to 'dish' and 'shovel' highlight the lack of skill she feels her role requires. She also feels that her £3.89 wage – the minimum wage at the time – makes her rank herself as someone who is at the bottom rung of the ladder financially. She feels foolish in her uniform, not special or respected at all.

b Take a range of personal responses from the students – some might include being unfulfilled, invisible, apathetic, empty, etc.

You should highlight to students that this first person narration allows the reader to become aware of Carla's innermost thoughts and feelings about her life – it gives the reader a more personal and intimate access into her character.

Third person narration

Third person narration is defined and exemplified. Students are also introduced to the terms 'omniscient' and 'restricted third person' while exploring the potential narrative freedom in terms of viewpoint that this form offers.

Activity 2 This activity asks students to consider the effect of restricted third person narration in 'Anil'.

Students should explore ideas such as how we, the reader, are allowed to become exposed to Anil's innermost thoughts and feelings, enabling us to identify with him and become further absorbed in the narrative and how the events have a personal impact upon him. Nurture discussion around this point and take all valid responses from students.

As students read the Anthology short stories, you could instigate discussion about whether the various points of view the writers have employed are effective in relation to the plot of each particular short story and whether students think alternative points of view would have been more appropriate.

Quick questions to ask about point of view/narrative voice

These bullet points are intended to help students consider and explore the narrative voice of a short story. They can be asked at the beginning of an analysis of narrative voice in order to focus students' attention or as a revision exercise to remind students of the sorts of things to be looking out for. Students are reminded to ask:

- if the story is narrated in the **first person** and whether this is effective
- if the story is narrated in the **third person** and whether this is **restricted** to one viewpoint
- whether the form of narration is **effective**.

Remind students to provide evidence from the text to support their conclusions regarding these points. You should encourage students to think about the effect of each of these points and to consider how it affects their interpretation of the short story as a whole.

Character

This section explores the different types of character that writers can create for their short stories and the various methods of characterisation, such as physical description, dialogue and action, and comments from other characters or the narrator, that a writer can use to reveal aspects of their character. Students are introduced to the roles of the protagonist and antagonist in a short story, and explore the differences between dynamic, static, flat and round characters.

Activity 1

kt Interactive activity: Character types

This activity asks students to assign a character type to its definition.

Students should respond as follows:

- Protagonist – The main character: the one with whom the reader's interest tends to centre.
- Antagonist – The character that is the force working against the main character: the one standing in the main character's way.
- Dynamic character – A character that is seen to be multi-dimensional and possibly complex: they will have a range of traits – good or bad.
- Static character – A character that changes very little, if at all: the one that largely remains constant in their beliefs, attitudes, behaviour and personality.
- Flat character – A character that is relatively simple and one-dimensional: they can be seen to represent a 'type' and be fairly stereotypical.
- Round character – A character that, during the course of the short story, undergoes a significant, lasting change: the one who evolves, learning something that changes them in a permanent way.

Activity 2 This activity builds on work covered in the previous activity. This activity is replicated on Worksheet 13a in the online resources.

Ensure that students provide evidence from the text to support their deductions. You may find that some students will have differing views – use this to explore their understanding of each character from the range of short stories covered.

Activity 3

kt Interactive activity: The short happy life of Frances Macomber

kt Interactive activity: A man and a woman

This activity asks students to consider the characterisation of Mrs Rutter in 'The Darkness Out There' and to write a comment about the character in 'On Seeing the 100% Perfect Girl One Beautiful April Morning'.

Take a range of valid responses from students. The following points could be raised to start their thinking:

- 'How can I approach her?' – the character is besotted with the girl and is desperate to find a way to speak to her.
- 'Ridiculous. I'd sound like an insurance salesman' – this shows how nervous the character is and how he does not want to make a fool of himself.

Quick questions to ask about character

These bullet points are intended to help students consider and explore the characters in a short story. They can be asked at the beginning of an analysis of character in order to focus students' attention or as a revision exercise to remind students of the sorts of things to be looking out for. Students are reminded to ask:

- what **type** of characters are presented
- what their **role** is in the short story
- what the reader **learns** from the characterisation
- if environments are **symbolic** of character.

Remind students to provide evidence from the text to support their conclusions regarding these points. You should encourage students to think about the effect of each of these points and to consider how it affects their interpretation of the short story as a whole.

Themes

kt Interactive activity: Short story themes

This section introduces the significance of a short story's theme and considers how themes can be developed. Students are encouraged to think about what ideas the writer could be wishing to express in their story, and to consider whether these views are clear or implicit. A list of common themes is provided as a starting point.

Activity 1 This activity asks students to think of other themes writers may explore.

Students could suggest the following examples: fear, duty, family, death, friendship and prejudice. Take a range of valid responses and encourage students to think creatively about the kinds of issues writers may wish to raise in their stories. You may wish to ask students to comment on which themes they are particularly interested in and why.

Activity 2 This activity asks students to closely examine the themes of a selection of Anthology short stories.

Allow students to work in pairs for this activity. Students may arrive at similar themes, but their evidence and view of the writer's opinion may differ. Be sure to monitor this and make certain that all opinions expressed are accurate. One example – following the prompts already provided in the Student Book – might be as follows:

- 'Compass and Torch': Family

Evidence: 'The boy was intent. Watching Dad. Watching what Dad is. Drinking it in: the essence of Dad.'

Writer's opinion: Baines wants the reader to see how much the relationship with the father means to the boy. He is desperate to get to know the father better and gain his affection.

This activity is replicated on Worksheet 13b in the online resources.

Activity 3 This activity is intended to strengthen student's understanding of how themes can be developed in a short story. Take valid additions from students and ask them to explain how their points assist in developing the theme of youth and age in 'The Darkness Out There'. Some sample additions include:

- Characterisation: reversal of stereotypes, Kerry does not behave in the way we might expect a teenage boy to behave.
- Setting: the lead-up to Mrs Rutter's cottage mirrors Sandra's carefree and simple life at this point.

Quick questions to ask about themes

These bullet points are intended to help students consider and explore the themes of a short story. They can be asked at the beginning of an analysis of theme in order to focus students' attention or as a revision exercise to remind students of the sorts of things to be looking out for. Students are reminded to ask:

- **what** the short story is about and how the reader knows this
- how characterisation and description **enhance** the theme
- if there is any **symbolism** and what it could mean.

Remind students to provide evidence from the text to support their conclusions regarding these points. You should encourage students to think about the effect of each of these points and to consider how it affects their interpretation of the short story as a whole.

Structure

(K) Interactive activity: Grabbing the reader's attention
(K) Interactive activity: Story endings

This section introduces students to the multiple ways in which a writer can organise their ideas and order the plot of the story. The pyramid plot structure is defined as a common model that writers employ – outlining the beginning, climax and end of a story's plot.

Activity 1 This activity asks students to consolidate their learning about the pyramid plot structure by identifying each stage of the narrative in the short stories they read.

Activity 2 This activity requires the students to define some features of structure.

Students should discover the following:

- Linear/chronological: the events occur in time sequence and run in a regular fashion from beginning to end.
- Flashbacks: the narrative jumps back to an incident that occurred in the past and allows readers to gain further insight into a character's motivations/the plot's progression.
- Fragmented narrative: the narrative is broken down and out of chronological order.

You could also introduce students to the following terms:

- Dual narrative: two viewpoints are presented in the narrative – these viewpoints may conflict.
- Multi-narrative: many different viewpoints are presented in the narrative.

Quick questions to ask about structure

These bullet points are intended to help students consider and explore the structure of a short story. They can be asked at the beginning of an analysis of structure in order to focus students' attention or as a revision exercise to remind students of the sorts of things to be looking out for. Students are reminded to ask:

- what is the **order** of events
- how the structure supports the **themes** of the short story.

Remind students to provide evidence from the text to support their conclusions regarding these points. You should encourage students to think about the effect of each of these points and to consider how it affects their interpretation of the short story as a whole.

Outcomes

(K) Interactive activity: Story terms 1
(K) Interactive activity: Story terms 2
(K) Interactive activity: Multiple-choice quiz – short stories

In this chapter students have learned how to approach their analysis of short stories by looking at the following elements:

- Setting
- Point of view
- Character
- Themes
- Structure

14 'The Darkness Out There'

 Analysis activity: Analysing 'The Darkness Out There'

AO focus

AO1: Respond to texts critically and imaginatively; select and evaluate relevant textual detail to illustrate and support interpretation.

AO2: Explain how language, structure and form contribute to writers' presentation of ideas, themes and settings.

In this chapter your students will:

- look at the following areas of analysis in relation to 'The Darkness Out There' by Penelope Lively from the short stories section of the Anthology: setting, point of view, character, themes and structure.

The key aspects of analysis that students covered in Chapter 13 of the Student Book: setting, point of view, character, theme and structure; now shape the progression of activities for this chapter, so that students are asked to answer questions on each of these areas in turn in relation to this one particular short story. It is hoped that this consistent and logical approach will increase students' confidence by equipping them with a clear method with which to apply their skills of analysis.

Additional resources

Worksheets:

- 14a: Activity 3
- 14b: Setting Activity 6
- 14c: Character Activity 18
- 14d: Character Activity 19

Getting started

This chapter looks in detail at 'The Darkness Out There' by Penelope Lively. The first part of the chapter is intended to help students to familiarise themselves with key points of content in the story and to think about some of the underlying issues before embarking on a full analysis. The first group of activities focus on stereotyping. The first two activities should be completed *before* students read 'The Darkness Out There'.

Activity 1 This activity asks students to consider the word 'stereotype' and its connotations.

All elements around this activity require a personal response from the students. Be sure to have discussed what the term 'stereotype' means. Ensure the students validate their responses with specific examples or reasoning.

Activity 2 This activity furthers students' thinking about stereotypes by applying it directly to characters in the short story.

All parts of this activity require the students to think about stereotypes surrounding two of the 'types' of character created within this short story. This enables you, as teacher, to identify and then highlight the stereotypes the author is both drawing our attention to and commenting/being critical of.

Activity 3 This activity asks students to consider what Lively is saying about stereotyping in 'The Darkness Out There'.

The activity takes students through a process of identifying certain stereotypes and also making judgements about such stereotyping. Some of the following points might prove good starting points for your approach to each part of this activity:

a Students may draw attention to the fact that they were shocked by Mrs Rutter's apparent ambivalence towards the death and suffering of the German soldier. Further to this, students may comment on the fact that Kerry appeared to be the one who presented an expected level of human morality, clearly being offended by Mrs Rutter's story.

b Alerted to examples such as that listed above, students may arrive at the fact that the author does indeed challenge stereotypes. Consider valid responses as to why.

c Two examples of characters themselves being guilty of stereotyping might include the following:

- The character Pat – she had described the people she was helping as 'the old folks' and had also drawn a rather insulting, stereotypical picture of 'a dear old bod with specs on the end of her nose and a shawl'

- Sandra – she makes the following sweeping statement: '*sort of gypsy types*'.

This activity is replicated on Worksheet 14a in the online resources.

Working through the chapter

Setting

Activity 4 This activity asks students to provide evidence of a modern-day setting.

This activity requires the students to analyse the text looking for textual clues that set this short story in the modern day. Allow only five minutes then share findings as a class. Take valid responses that use exemplification. Some examples include:

- 'People with platinum highlights and spike-heel suede boots.'

- '… lying on your stomach at home on the hearth rug watching telly with the curtains drawn …'

Activity 5 This activity aims to help students to contextualise Mrs Rutter's tale by considering life during the Second World War.

For this activity, students are encouraged to think about the VAD. In turn, students should hopefully take on board, and acknowledge, the care of such volunteer workers during the war years. This should perhaps only serve to highlight and contrast their understanding of Mrs Rutter and her sister's apparent cold and heartless behaviour.

Activity 6 This activity furthers students' knowledge of wartime by focusing their attention on detail in the text.

This activity will require students to carefully track and highlight all evidence that tells the reader something about the life people lived during the Second World War. The grid provided encourages students to find specific textual evidence. Share findings and gather as a class. Some examples include:

Life during Second World War	Evidence from the text
Many men were sent to Belgium in the early stages of the war and some did not come back.	'"Killed in the war, dear. Right at the start. He was in one of the first campaigns, in Belgium, and he never came back."'
Some of the German planes were called Messerschmitts.	'She chuckled. "I saw it come down all right." "What was it?" said the boy. "Messerschmitt?" "How would I know that, dear? I don't know anything about aeroplanes."'

This activity is replicated on Worksheet 14b in the online resources.

Activity 7 This activity focuses students' attention on the contrast in atmosphere generated by the changing setting.

a Students should match the extracts as follows:

Beginning: '… she walked through flowers, the girl, ox-eye daisies and vetch and cow parsley …'

Middle: '… you didn't know who there might be around, in woods and places …'

End: '… you glimpsed darkness, an inescapable darkness.'

b Students should note that the move from a sunny and idyllic setting to a dark and sinister one reflects the course of the plot, that Sandra learns something that changes her view of her surroundings. Students should comment on the now much more negative and unsettled feeling that the shocked Sandra experiences on her way home.

Again, this activity will require the students to carefully track and highlight evidence that covers the focus for this question. It is important that students not only provide the textual evidence, but also develop their inference and deduction skills by trying to interpret author intention. Another example signifying a change in setting is provided below, should you need to model one:

Line 65: 'she walked through the thicker grass by the hedge and felt it drag at her legs …'

The softness and lightness of nature, previously alluded to has gone. We now have a heavy, thicker, dense and foreboding element to the nature she is almost 'wading' through. The grass is almost personified as it appears to 'pull' at her legs. Its hold is quite uninviting, almost threatening.

Activity 8 This activity draws students' attention to the references to the beauty of nature.

Students should select the third bullet point.

For this activity, encourage students to think about the life/appearance and cycle of elements of nature; the natural habitat is forever changing and is not always how it first appears. Support students' further linkage with how their first view of Mrs Rutter (and the initial stereotypes formed) changes as the plot progresses – appearance is not always the reality.

Point of view

Activity 9 This activity asks students to identify the viewpoint.

This activity allows you to explore and consolidate student understanding of third person viewpoint. The reader is presented with the viewpoint of Sandra. Three examples include:

- line 35 – 'she thought suddenly of blank-eyed helmeted heads ...'
- line 132 – 'she wished there was Susie to have a giggle with, not just that Kerry Stevens.'
- line 369 – 'and she would hear, she thought, always, for a long time anyway, that voice.'

Activity 10 This activity asks students to consider Lively's intention in creating this type of narration.

For this activity, students will need to form and substantiate their own opinions of the author's decision to craft this short story in the third person. Students could select either of the first two bullet points as both can be supported. As an extension activity, you could ask students to experiment with rewriting a paragraph of the story in the first person and to consider how this affects the reader's interpretation.

Activity 11 This activity encourages students to consider the effect of alternative viewpoints.

For this activity, students will need to think about the story from Mrs Rutter's viewpoint. One possible way of approaching this activity is to get students to brainstorm their ideas on a sheet of paper, logging all they know about Mrs Rutter on the day of the visit – but also what they might think she feels at certain points during the visit. Students should acknowledge Mrs Rutter's loneliness, her personal emotional link to the event of the German soldier's death and the impact upon her as a result of the death of her husband during the war. Encourage students to think about how the tone of the story may have differed if the reader was presented with the viewpoint of Mrs Rutter – and how this might have affected their interpretation. Take a range of valid responses from the students, encouraging them to cite textual evidence.

Character

Activity 12 This activity asks students to think about why Lively has chosen to begin and close her story with the character of Sandra.

Take a range of personal responses to this question. One possible student response may focus on the fact that the short story beginning and ending with Sandra allows us, as the reader, to fully witness the journey she has been on and the impact it has evidently had on her life. As a result, the messages become heightened.

Activity 13 This activity explores Sandra's journey in the story.

This activity allows students to explore the idea that Sandra appears to have gone on a journey from being a girl to becoming a woman in the fact that she is starting to lose her innocent, naïve

view of life. The incident at Mrs Rutter's cottage has meant that she does not feel as secure in her surroundings as she once did. She now realises that there is often more in life to be considered than what might at first appear. Encourage students to explore both extracts and respond appropriately.

Activity 14 This activity looks at an example of Lively's characterisation of Sandra.

For this activity, place the phrase in the centre of the whiteboard, and ask students to come to the front of the class and brainstorm ideas around the significance of a statement such as 'keeping to the track'. Students may possibly arrive at the fact that when we meet Sandra, her life appears to be mundane and safe. She seems pleased by the little things in life and her dreams are quite simple and stereotypical. The statement could symbolise the fact that Sandra does not wander from 'the track' in life; she lacks adventure, excitement, wonder and question.

Activity 15 This activity asks students to describe Sandra at both the beginning and end of the story.

This activity requires a personal response from your students. Take a range of valid responses, sharing many with the class as a whole. Encourage validation by making textual reference where necessary. Students may suggest that Sandra is naïve, innocent and safe as she walks to the house and wiser, shocked and disturbed as she walks away from it.

Activity 16 This activity focuses on Kerry's reaction to Mrs Rutter's story.

This activity is encouraging students to look at the events from the viewpoint of Kerry, trying to understand his initial reaction to the information Mrs Rutter has revealed. Support student/ class discussion around this point. One possible interpretation might centre around how the events of history and society can influence our views and actions. Had Kerry been immersed in the conflict and horror of war, had he lost members of his family and loved ones, then might his views have been different? Might his disgust at Mrs Rutter's actions have been diluted? Ask students to back up the assertions they make. Is Lively perhaps implying that we shouldn't feel as Kerry does, but that we should try to be open to 'another side to the story' before we make our judgements?

Activity 17 This activity looks at the impression generated of Kerry in the story.

This activity requires a personal response from the students and allows them to explore their own stereotypes and prejudices. Encourage students to explain if and how their impressions of Kerry change as the narrative develops.

Activity 18 This activity focuses students' attention on the descriptions provided of Mrs Rutter and her house.

Again, this activity requires students' personal response as the result of close tracking and highlighting of textual detail. Students should build on, and add to, the example already supplied in the Student Book. If some students are perhaps struggling as to where to find such detail, initially direct them as a starting point to lines 97–122 and lines 141–4. Students should think about employing the PEE (Point, Evidence, Explanation) approach to structuring their paragraphs.

This activity is replicated on Worksheet 14c in the online resources.

Activity 19 This activity looks at some further examples of Lively's characterisation.

This activity allows the students to look at the inferences implied through certain examples of text in relation to particular characters. Encourage the students to be as thorough and detailed as they can be with their explanation. A starting point for those students who might find this hard has been begun below:

Character	Evidence	Explanation
Mrs Rutter	'the walls were cluttered with old calendars'	Holding on to the past, aware of time and its passing, 'cluttered' implies a lack of clarity, structure, order to her life – it is as though she has given up on a future.
Kerry	'his shirt clung to his shoulder blades, damp with sweat...'	Hardworking, reliable, focused.
Sandra	'one day, this year, next year, sometime, she would go to places like on travel brochures...'	Lacks focus and impetus, lives in a dream world but lacks the determination to make things happen.
Pat Hammond	'Pat had done the notice...a jokey cartoon drawing of a dear old bod with specs on the end of her nose and a shawl...'	Quite insulting and condescending, lacking in a sense of appropriateness.

This activity is replicated on Worksheet 14d in the online resources.

Activity 20 This activity focuses on Lively's use of simile and metaphor in her characterisation.

For this activity, students will need to be familiar with both language devices 'metaphor' and 'simile'. Perhaps use this activity as a revisit/consolidation of both terms. Take all valid interpretations of examples provided by the students. If your students are finding it hard to locate any, perhaps you could direct them to the following as a starting point:

- Line 97 – 'a cottage-loaf of a woman'
- Line 98 – 'a creamy smiling pool of a face'
- Line 111 – 'her eyes investigated, quick as mice'.

Encourage students to consider the effect of such imagery.

Activity 21 This activity encourages students to make a personal response to the story's revelation and to think about the writer's intention.

This activity encourages students to form their own views surrounding the incident of Mrs Rutter leaving and allowing the young German soldier to die. Take a range of responses, always promoting the fact that students need to refer to textual evidence to validate and justify their own point of view.

Stretch yourself These activities require students to empathise with appointed characters from this short story, using description and detail to build aspects of character. Take a range of responses and listen as a class.

Themes

Activity 22 This activity asks students to consider the many contrasts present in 'The Darkness Out There'.

For this activity, allow the students to explore the theme of contrasts. A starting point of 'youth and age' has been provided in the Student Book. Should any of your groups of students find this activity difficult, you could perhaps provide some of the following to springboard discussion:

- good/bad
- lies/honesty
- past/present (future)
- appearance/reality
- darkness/light.

Examples provided here are not exhaustive.

Activity 23 This activity looks at the use of the word 'darkness' in the story.

Students should explore the significance of the repeated 'dark' and 'darkness' given within this short story. Possible interpretations might focus on:

- The darkness implies the distinction between appearance and reality – that we do not always see the reality/aspects of reality can often lay under the surface, as if in darkness.

- The darkness links metaphorically to evil/ good – the darkness implying the evil aspects of human nature and life.

Remind students that this is immediately brought to the reader's attention in the title.

Structure

Activity 24 This activity is a plot sequencing activity.

Use this activity as a way of consolidating students' understanding of the narrative and its structure. Work with the class as a whole for this activity, ensuring students have the correct ordering. The order should be as follows:

1 Sandra walks to Mrs Rutter's house. She bumps into Kerry on the way.

2 Sandra helps Mrs Rutter with some chores inside her cottage. Mrs Rutter and Sandra talk.

3 Mrs Rutter tells both Sandra and Kerry about her tale regarding the German soldiers.

4 Kerry feels he must leave the cottage. His view and opinion of Mrs Rutter has changed dramatically.

5 Sandra follows Kerry and they walk away from the house.

Outcomes

Interactive activity: Responding to 'The Darkness Out There'

In this chapter students have learned how to:

- approach their analysis of 'The Darkness Out There' by looking at the following elements: setting, point of view, character, theme and structure

- consider the context of 'The Darkness Out There'

- think about the language and imagery the writer has used

- explore the meaning of the short story and consider the writer's intentions

- make a personal response to short stories.

15 'Compass and Torch'

Analysis activity: Analysing 'Compass and Torch'

Viewpoints activity: 'Compass and Torch'

AO focus

AO1: Respond to texts critically and imaginatively; select and evaluate relevant textual detail to illustrate and support interpretation.

AO2: Explain how language, structure and form contribute to writers' presentation of ideas, themes and settings.

In this chapter your students will:

- look at the following areas of analysis in relation to 'Compass and Torch' by Elizabeth Baines: setting, point of view, character, themes and structure.

In this chapter, students analyse 'Compass and Torch' by Elizabeth Baines from the short stories section of the Anthology. The key aspects of analysis that students covered in Chapter 13 of the Student Book: setting, point of view, character, theme and structure, now shape the progression of activities for this chapter, so that students are asked to answer questions on each of these areas in turn in relation to one particular short story. It is hoped that this consistent and logical approach will increase students' confidence by equipping them with a clear method with which to apply their skills of analysis.

Additional resources

Worksheets:

- 15a: Point of view Activity 10

Getting started

This chapter looks in detail at 'Compass and Torch' by Elizabeth Baines. The first part of the chapter is intended to help students to familiarise themselves with key points of content in the story and to think about some of the underlying issues before embarking on a full analysis. The first group of activities focus on family trips. The first three activities should be completed *before* students read 'Compass and Torch'.

Activity 1 This activity asks students to discuss the reasons why people may take camping trips.

Take a range of valid and appropriate responses from your students, encouraging explanation.

Activity 2 This activity asks students to comment on some images of a father and son.

This is an introductory activity that encourages the students to think about the relationship between father and son before they look closely at the father and son relationship presented in 'Compass and Torch'. They are asked to rank order a list of words to describe each of the scenes. Take a range of appropriate orders, plus explanation and reasoning, from your students.

Activity 3 This activity asks students to think about their responses to Activity 2 after reading 'Compass and Torch'.

Students should also explore the symbolic aspect of the camping trip; that the pair have been, and appear still to be, 'camping' in each other's lives.

Working through the chapter

Setting

Activity 4 This activity asks students to identify evidence of setting in terms of time and place.

Students are encouraged to look at description and detail of setting in this activity. There are numerous examples of textual evidence that supports the idea that this is in a modern-day setting. Encourage your students to track and highlight key examples. Some examples might touch on references to the car, the boy's rucksack and his torch.

Activity 5 This activity focuses students' attention on the horse in the story.

Students should use this activity to analyse the possible symbolism of the horses. The writer herself has stated that at first she was initially capturing events that she actually saw on an outing with her husband and not intentionally symbolising points.

However, it is valid to look at the horses with symbolism, as Baines herself states that she eventually saw how events and points could become symbolic and she added to and enhanced these points. We, as the reader are only too aware of the actions of the horses; however, the father and son are clearly not. This only serves to heighten the fact that they are too caught up in their fraught and fractured relationship to notice the beauty around them. Further to this, students might pick up on the fact that the horses appear to have a sensitive, soft and intuitive nature: something that the boy and more intently, the father, are suppressing. Baines herself has further suggested that the 'wild fringed eyes' represent the boy's unconscious acknowledgment of the emotions about his father he will learn to turn a blind eye to, and that the thudding hooves further represent his beating heart, the seat of the grief for his father which he will learn to suppress.

Activity 6 This activity focuses on Baines' use of simile and metaphor in the short story.

In exploring the first simile, students might provide responses that touch on the obvious, that the parting of the clouds is like the parting of curtains, letting in light, brightening up the day/surroundings. The symbolism could refer to the opening up of the father/son relationship – that it is now open, in view, nothing hidden, nothing standing between them; a potential fresh start like the start of a new day.

The extract provided in the second half of the question again reflects how distracted and caught up in the emotional strain the father and son are. They are described as being 'too focused on their goal' to stop and take in the beauty that surrounds them. The sense of urgency here makes the reader feel uneasy – why doesn't the father simply relax and enjoy the time with his son? The 'still black mirror of lake' is a striking metaphor and indicates that the natural world is 'reflecting' the difficulties in their relationship ('black' mirror adds a further note of unease).

Some other examples of metaphor or simile that students might focus on include 'like heaving carcasses asleep' and 'snaking wall'. Ensure that students are focused on the effect of such techniques.

Activity 7 This activity asks students to examine an annotated part of the text which indicates that the setting enforces a sense of confusion and disorder.

This activity requires the students to track and trace examples of detail that indicate that things might not be what they seem. Use the example annotations provided in the Student Book to model to students and explain textual clues and possible inferences.

Point of view

Activity 8 This activity asks students to identify the viewpoint in 'Compass and Torch'.

Students should use this activity to consolidate their understanding of viewpoint from their learning in Chapter 13. Take responses from students ensuring they understand that we are

being presented with this narrative largely from the viewpoint of the young boy/son.

Activity 9 This activity asks students to consider the effect of writing in the third person.

Students may offer a range of possible personal responses to this activity. Ask students to explain their reasons in full. Examples that might be supplied could touch on the following:

- If the narrative was in the first person from the son's point of view, the reader might not get the full emotional insight into the child owing to his inability to express his emotions fully, or the fact that he might be biased in not seeing his father's faults/limitations.

- We are able to have glimpses of the feelings of other characters in the third person which helps to highlight the tragedy of this failing relationship.

Activity 10 This activity focuses students' attention on the feelings of several characters in the story at various points.

This activity is further exploring the idea of point of view. Allow the students to work with a partner, brainstorming the incidents highlighted and exploring how different characters might possibly interpret/feel about it. Students will be strengthening their skills of empathy, inference and deduction. Share and discuss findings as a class. The following could be suggested:

The incident	The young boy	The father	The mother
The fact that the father has not spent time with his son for the past four months.	Sad as he misses his father and doesn't understand why he doesn't spend more time with him.	Guilt that he has been neglectful. Worried that he has left it too long to reconnect with his son.	Angry and upset with the father and worried for her son.
The prospect of going on the camping trip.	Excited as he has not seen his father in so long.	Concerned that it will not be enough to make up for his actions. Worried that it will go wrong.	Concerned for her son as he is excited and she thinks he will only be disappointed. Annoyed with the father for turning up in this way when he has been absent for a while.

The incident	The young boy	The father	The mother
Realising the boy and the father have both brought torches.	Initially worried but then excited because they can light up more.	Grateful to have something to talk about with his son.	Not involved.
The boy and father each forgetting their compass.	Dismayed at first but then relieved that they have both forgotten one.	Annoyed with himself but attempts to brush it off.	Not involved.

This activity is replicated on Worksheet 15a in the online resources.

Activity 11 This activity asks students to consider the mood created in the short story.

This activity will require a personal response from the students. Share and discuss findings as a class. Students are likely to suggest that the mood is anxious, tense and lonely. Ask students to explain their choices.

Character

Activity 12 This activity asks students to consider the lack of names in the narrative.

This activity is exploring aspects of characterisation.

a   The only character referred to by name is Jim, the mother's new partner.

b   The other characters are referred to according to their role in the family.

Some possible starting points for why this is might include:

- No names symbolises the fact that this could be any family, and is probably representative of many families.

- No names could be symbolic of the fact that each person has indeed lost their identity as a result of the parents' split – they have somehow lost who they are or who they should be.

- The fact that we merely have the 'roles' instead of the specific names could symbolise the fact that each needs to remember the duties/expectation of their roles. The young boy isn't allowed to merely be the son – he is shouldering the unfair burden and responsibilities that such a separation has presented him with.

Activity 13 This activity looks in detail at how the boy is referred to in the text.

Encourage the students to arrive at possible interpretations that focus on the 'change' within the father. This camping trip is helping the father to bond with his son. The father is starting to take responsibility and 'ownership' of **his** role and **his** son's needs. The shift is positive as it occurs, but still raises questions as to whether it will be sustained. The boy is now presented as 'belonging'.

Activity 14 This activity focuses students' attention on a particular line which gives the reader an insight into how the boy feels about his father.

This activity will explore the fact that the boy seems intently focused on his father – almost scared to take his eyes off his father in case he disappears or leaves. He appears to be relishing the time they have together, absorbing every minute and detail. It could further highlight the point that he has been 'starved' of such encounters. He is 'drinking' the time they have together as one would drink to live; it is extremely important to the son. Does this also mean however, that the boy is likewise aware that there may be an end to this – that he has to savour these moments, as they may not last? Take a range of valid personal responses that similarly explore such approaches to the extract.

Activity 15 This activity asks students to consider the symbolism of the compass and torch in the story.

Students should approach this task on two levels. Initially, they should explore the importance for the compass and torch to the little boy; they are objects of importance for the trip going successfully. Symbolically, the two might be seen to signify the fact that the father has lost direction and focus in his relationship with his son. Something is needed to put them back on the path and to point them in the right direction. Building on this, students may also offer the fact that the compass and torch further signify the lack of emotional equipment that has been taken/remembered for this trip/ situation. Take valid responses, with explanation, from the students.

Stretch yourself This activity further reinforces students understanding of characterisation and, more specifically, the point of view/feelings potentially experienced by the son in this short story.

Activity 16 This activity looks in detail at the father's awareness of his son.

This activity will require students to track the short story for evidence that shows the father does not 'know' his son. Ask students to share their findings with the whole class, perhaps logging them on the whiteboard as you work your way through the text. Take personal responses as to how this makes the students feel; these responses should be substantiated with explanation.

Activity 17 This activity looks at Baines' use of modifiers in her characterisation of the father.

There are a number of examples in this story of modifiers being used to describe the father. Further to the examples supplied in the Student Book, model the following to the students:

- 'pushing the gate with one arm, <u>abruptly</u>'
- 'driving the car <u>quickly</u>, <u>efficiently</u> through the gate'
- '<u>gratefully</u> caught on a wave of triumph'
- 'says with <u>robust</u> authority'
- 'The man <u>gently</u> takes away the torch'

Take a range of examples and explanations from the students, perhaps further highlighting the fact that the description of the father changes as we progress through the narrative, i.e. from 'abruptly' to 'gently' as shown above.

Activity 18 This activity requires students to make a personal response about the father.

This activity requires the students to focus their attention on the father, building on their skills of empathy, inference and deduction. Take a range of valid, personal responses from the students, reinforcing their need to explain and justify.

Stretch yourself This activity further builds on the analysis of character. You could use the role-play as an opportunity to make a formal assessment for the drama aspect of the Speaking and Listening assessments.

Themes

Activity 19 This activity asks students to look at the use of contrast in 'Compass and Torch'.

a In addition to the child/adult and love/hate contrasts, students could suggest that the story contains the following:

- man/nature
- close relationships/loneliness
- mother/father.

b Students are now asked to focus on one of the key contrasts they have identified and to log all the evidence they can find to support it. This will reinforce with students the need to back up their arguments with evidence from the text.

Activity 20 This activity asks students to look closely at the key relationships in the story.

Ask students to copy this diagram onto a sheet of A3 paper, allowing time and space to highlight the similarities and differences between the three major characters: the son, the mum and the dad. This activity will allow students to explore the dynamics of the relationships and further appreciate aspects that have broken down. To consolidate, project this diagram onto your whiteboard and asks students to plot and log their findings.

Activity 21 This activity focuses students' attention on Baines's use of juxtaposition.

For this activity, students are encouraged to take their analysis of characters and relationships and to apply it to that of the father and the stepfather, Jim.

a For the first part to this activity, ask students to focus on the juxtaposing of Jim with the dad. Students should offer personal responses as to whether they feel this works, explaining their views with a partner. Students may touch on the consistency, presence and ongoing security of one (Jim) contrasting and thereby reinforcing the inconsistency and absence of the other (the dad).

b The answers to the latter part of this activity are:

- Dad: 'gratefully caught on a wave of triumph', 'says with robust authority', 'gently takes away the torch', 'own anxiety began to mount', 'bats her away'.
- Jim: 'gently twisted the barrel', 'asked kindly', 'said pointedly approving'.

Structure

Activity 22 This activity asks students to consider the opening of 'Compass and Torch'.

Take a range of personal responses from the students. They should look at the phrase as perhaps symbolic – there is an obvious end to the journey – or indeed a barrier to overcome. The fact that we are faced with a gate and not a wall further implies that there might be hope, should the right steps be taken to open the gate and move on into the next stage of their journey/their life together. The latter is only one possible reading; encourage students to explore this in more detail.

Activity 23 This activity focuses students' attention on the way that Baines begins many of her sentences.

This activity encourages the students to examine the fact that we are reading this from the primary viewpoint of the son.

a The boy is engrossed by his father and the sentences highlight how everything he thinks and does is a reaction to the father. The reader is allowed to get a clear impression of how the father affects the boy.

b The short, simple sentences indicate that the emotions in this story are very raw and perhaps highlight the sad mood as the boy only wants love and attention and struggles to get it.

Activity 24 This activity draws students' attention to the reference to the horse.

Ask students to consider the sentence provided in this task. Students may offer a range of responses that cover some of the following aspects:

- The fact that the sentence is pre-empted by the phrase 'a display which could easily fascinate an eight year old boy ...' is poignant here. We have further evidence of the fact that the boy is so caught up in pleasing his father that he is not relaxed or behaving as a healthy eight-year-old boy might. He is oblivious to events around him, focused only on the camping trip and their time together.

- The event is shocking, which perhaps further signifies the shocking state of the relationship between father and son displayed in this narrative.

Take a range of valid personal responses from the students, substantiated by explanation and, where possible, evidence.

Activity 25 This activity looks at Baines's use of flashbacks in the narrative.

a One possible reason for the inclusion of flashbacks might focus on the fact that they offer detail and background to the camping trip. We need a glimpse of this to realise the lack of presence of the father to date, the conflict that is present between the father and mother and the emotional need and want of the son to be with his father and feel loved and

wanted by him. The flashbacks put into context his intent and intensity on the trip itself. Be sure students explore the structure and offer personal reasons as to why Baines has crafted it in such a way. Do they feel the flashbacks are effective?

b This activity is not only focusing on narrative structure but it is closely linked to characterisation.

Take a range of personal responses from the students. One suggestion might be that we are able to see the antagonism between the mother and father, which could offer some explanation as to why the father has kept away. Students might also offer the fact that the boy feels that he wants to bond with his father as he is in fear of losing him/ having him replaced by Jim.

c This activity requires personal responses, with explanation, from the students. You could collate responses from students and write them on the board. Students could then vote on which flashback they would most like to see in the story and they could each write this flashback.

Outcomes

In this chapter students have learned how to:

- approach their analysis of 'Compass and Torch' by looking at the following elements: setting, point of view, character, theme and structure

- consider the context of 'Compass and Torch'

- think about the language and imagery the writer has used

- explore the meaning of the short story and consider the writer's intentions

- make a personal response to short stories.

'Anil'

🔂 Interactive activity: Analysing 'Anil'

AO focus

AO1: Respond to texts critically and imaginatively; select and evaluate relevant textual detail to illustrate and support interpretation.

AO2: Explain how language, structure and form contribute to writers' presentation of ideas, themes and settings.

In this chapter your students will:

● look at the following areas of analysis in relation to 'Anil' by Ridjal Noor: setting, point of view, character, themes and structure.

In this chapter, students analyse 'Anil' by Ridjal Noor from the short stories Anthology. The key aspects of analysis that students covered in Chapter 13 of the Student Book: setting, point of view, character, theme and structure, now shape the progression of activities for this chapter, so that students are asked to answer questions on each of these areas in turn in relation to a particular short story. It is hoped that this consistent and logical approach will increase students' confidence by equipping them with a clear method with which to apply their skills of analysis.

Additional resources

Worksheets:

● 16a: Activity 2
● 16b: Character Activity 9
● 16c: Character Activity 14
● 16d: Structure Activity 19

Getting started

Introduction

This chapter looks in detail at 'Anil' by Ridjal Noor. The first part of the chapter is intended to help students to familiarise themselves with key points of content in the story and to think about some of the underlying issues before embarking on a full analysis. The first group of activities focus on aspects of culture that the story presents. The first two activities should be completed before students read 'Anil'.

In addition to the guidance below on the activities provided in the Student Book, the following activities can be used to help students understand the idea and significance of culture prior to their study of 'Anil'. The conclusions students draw here will help to strengthen their understanding of contextual factors in short stories generally.

● Ask students to make a list of factors that can influence a person's culture, for example gender and nationality.

● Students should then prioritise three main factors that they think create or influence cultures.

● What factors determine culture? Are students interested in them all? Do they feel they can change any aspects of their culture?

● Students can go on to describe their culture, sharing their description with someone else in the class. Are their descriptions similar?

The following table shows definitions for some terms students may be unfamiliar with in 'Anil'. You could mix the definitions up and ask students to match the correct one to each word.

Words	Definitions
Appa	Father
Amma	Mother
Thali	A necklace given instead of a wedding ring
Omnipresent	Present in all places at the same time
Pesase	Ghost
Rattan	Leaves from climbing palms that have tough stems that can make furniture
Pyre	A pile of wood used for cremating a corpse

Activity 1 This activity asks students to complete a spider diagram with everything they know about Malaysia – the setting of 'Anil'.

This activity gives students the opportunity to discuss their knowledge of this country in groups. Students will have differing levels of starting knowledge so encourage them to write down any questions they would like to know the answer to. Collate students' responses on the board. If students struggle, the following facts could be offered:

● Malaysia is in Asia, close to Thailand and Singapore.

● The capital of Malaysia is Kuala Lumpur.

● It has a tropical climate and experiences monsoons.

- Exports include rubber, cocoa, pineapple and tobacco.
- The official religion is Islam.
- It is a developing country but is rapidly progressing in terms of economy and education.
- Rice and noodles are staple foods.
- The official language is Malay.

Activity 2 This activity asks students to consider the culture of Malaysia.

Encourage students to record the differences in lifestyle in a table. You could use some of the general questions about culture above to aid students' thinking. You could return to their responses after reading 'Anil' to see whether students wish to add or remove any of the points they made.

This activity is replicated on Worksheet 16a in the online resources.

Working through the chapter

Setting

Activity 3 This activity asks students to study the annotation provided of the opening of 'Anil'.

Encourage students to consider the details that grab the reader's attention and establish the setting. The annotations highlight some of the indicators that tell the reader this is set in a poor foreign country and emphasises the threatening tone which sets the scene for the action which is to follow.

The following points suggest that the story is not set in the UK:

- the mosquitoes
- the temperature in March
- the huts
- the foreign names.

The following points suggest that the setting is afflicted by poverty:

- the huts
- their simple dreams – a profitable harvest, a new cow, a sewing machine.

Activity 4 This activity looks in detail at the dreams of the villagers and what these say about their lives.

'The villagers do not have much to look forward to' is the most appropriate answer. Encourage students to provide evidence from the text to support the response they give.

Activity 5 This activity asks students to closely study an annotated section of the text from the beginning of the story.

This passage draws students' attention to the effect of the darkness. In setting the opening sections of his story in the dark, Noor heightens the sense of tension and drama which the reader can already infer from the references to violence and fear.

a   The dark creates an atmosphere of fear for the reader because we view it through Anil's eyes. It is very quiet and eerie. Evil things can occur and be concealed by the dark.

b   Anil is afraid of the dark. He daren't go outside to the toilet alone and he imagines ghosts waiting for him.

Activity 6 This activity asks for a personal response from students to the setting that Noor establishes.

Students are likely to say that the village is unappealing. There are no luxuries or home comforts that we take for granted such as houses and inside toilets. It is very hot and there are mosquitoes. It is dark and intimidating. There does not appear to be any education or ambition and people struggle through their daily lives.

Point of view

Activity 7 This activity focuses students' attention on the point of view of the story.

The story is written from Anil's point of view as the title suggests. We see things – such as the hanging of the woman – through Anil's eyes. The reader experiences the realisation of what is happening with Anil. For example, 'It wasn't a white cloth, it was a woman dressed in white, her long black hair synonymous with the darkness and strewn across her face. They were hanging a woman.'

Activity 8 This activity draws students' attention to the ways in which Noor uses descriptive language which appeals to the reader's senses.

There are many examples of what Anil sees and hears. Here are a few:

- Anil sees: a star; the large ghostly tree that grew in front of the hut; the bruise on his mother's shoulder; his father fall to his knees.
- Anil hears: the sound of the crickets crying out to each other; a voice hissing 'Marimuthu!'; a noisy commotion outside the hut; the wail of the train.

This descriptive detail allows the reader to truly immerse themselves in Anil's perspective.

Character

Activity 9 This activity asks students to think about what they know about Anil and how his life differs from theirs.

a   Some ideas for a fact file on Anil are that:

- he is seven
- his father is Ragunathan
- his mother and father worked for the headman
- his father has hit him
- he has dreams
- he witnesses a murder
- he is honest.

b   This requires a personal response but students should focus particularly on the differences in education, home and family life.

You could ask students what they feel for Anil. Do they feel sympathy? Can they relate to him in any way? Are they keen to find out what happens to him?

This activity is replicated on Worksheet 16b in the online resources.

Activity 10 This activity draws students' attention to Anil's childlike innocence and imagination.

Students need to examine the text closely in order to respond. Remind students to think about the contrast that is presented between Anil's innocence and the horror that unfolds. Some examples are:

- 'It was a tree that ate little children.' This shows his childlike innocence as he believes the stories that he has heard and he does not question their validity.

- 'Expecting a ghastly face to emerge at the window and send him screaming his head off.' This is an example of how children's imaginations can be very vivid and frightening. He anticipates seeing a scary face but of course he actually witnesses something far worse and real.

- '... he believed in the magical wonders of life.' This exemplifies how children are often optimistic and positive – they believe in magic and dreams. This contrasts with the harsh reality of what he witnesses.

Activity 11 This activity asks students to explore Anil's reaction to the horror that he witnesses.

a   Students should select the last bullet point. Another example of fear is: 'Anil's heart stilled for a moment, caught in a shocking revelation.' This quotation reveals Anil's sheer horror as he realises that it isn't a cloth the men are carrying but a woman. His fear is so great that it feels as though his heart has stopped briefly.

b   Noor repeats the phrase, 'If there was something out there' to build suspense. 'Something' is an 'empty' word which increases the suspense as the reader wants to know what that 'something' could be.

c   Some other character's reactions are given but the narrative mostly focuses on Anil's response. Seen through a child's eyes, the events seem even more frightening and uncontrollable.

Activity 12 This activity asks students to think about Noor's opinion about Anil's father.

Noor is possibly justifying Anil's father's decision not to expose the truth. He is highlighting the opportunities that his father did not have so the reader can see why he chooses to send Anil away. The chance to help his son break out of the life that is destined for him in the village is too appealing. Also, Noor is suggesting that Anil's father has only ever been taught to serve his headman so he does not have the intelligence to question his orders. Ensure that students support whichever point they select with evidence from the text.

Activity 13 This activity looks at the motivations of Anil's father.

a   Take a range of responses from the class. Students may suggest that it would be difficult for him to disobey the headman but the opportunity for Anil to be educated would also have been attractive to any father in the village.

b   Encourage students to debate these points in turn by referring to evidence from the text itself.

Activity 14 This activity asks students to consider how a selection of characters feels at the end of the story. Students could suggest the following:

Character	Feeling	Evidence
Anil	Devastated, apprehensive, lonely and confused.	'Anil sat in his train seat and cried.' 'Where am I going?'
Appa	Guilty and distressed.	'Someday you will see that it is for your own good.' 'He saw his father fall to his knees, a bent despaired figure that had just let go of his only son.'
Marimuthu	Relaxed, relieved.	'He heaved a sigh of relief.'

This activity is replicated on Worksheet 16c in the online resources.

Stretch yourself This activity encourages students to think creatively and to deeply consider the motivations of the characters in 'Anil'. Some interesting characters to explore include Appa, Marimuthu and Anil himself.

Themes

Activity 15 This activity asks students to suggest the themes that are present in 'Anil'.

Some suggestions are: truth, power, poverty. For each theme, ask students to provide a quote from the text to support it.

Activity 16 This activity looks at the theme of violence in the story.

a This part of the activity encourages students to find textual evidence to support different points. The following could be suggested by students:

- Anil's father is abusive towards his family – 'Anil saw the bruise on her shoulder, where Appa, returning home drunk last night, had hit her.'

- The description of the hanging of the woman is graphic – 'After a few moments, the body of the woman lay limp, swaying from side to side and twirling sadistically to face east and then west and then east again.'

- The atmosphere in the village is tense and frightening – 'Right now, he dared not even think of the reason why he would not return.'

b The metaphor evokes a sense of fear and tension owing to the negative associations with mosquitoes and terrorism. 'Terrorism' and 'reign' could also relate to the power of the headman. The village is obviously quite an intimidating place at night for Anil.

c Students could select one of the quotes from the first part of this activity and write a comment about the effect that it has on the reader.

d This question requires a personal response from students but many students may be shocked by the extreme nature of the violence. Noor's intention here is to show the harsh contrast between growing up in the United Kingdom and Malaysia.

Activity 17 This activity looks at the theme of childhood in the story.

a The passage suggests that although the father and son did not previously show affection towards each other, they are both distraught by the separation. Anil cries alone on the train and his father falls to his knees.

b This requires a personal response. Previous questions should have helped pupils to form an opinion of the father and some may think that the violence he has shown towards Anil previously suggests he does not care much for him; they may therefore be surprised to see his grief at the end of the story. However, as his father, some students may feel his reaction is to be expected.

Stretch yourself This activity requires students to think creatively and to try and understand the father's intentions and concerns. You may get a variety of responses from students but always ensure that they can support the comments they have written with sustained evidence from the text.

Activity 18 This activity asks students to consider whether Anil is happy in the village.

Anil did not appear to be happy living in the village as he did not dare to go to the toilet alone; he was obviously frightened. He believed stories that increased his fear such as 'It was a tree that ate little children.' Also, he dared not to wake his father as he decided that 'he did not need a walloping at this time of night.' It was a harsh childhood but Anil would not have known any different, which is why he still states that he does not want to leave. He loves his parents and is afraid to experience the unknown as he is so young and has never experienced an alternative lifestyle. Either of the last two bullet points can be supported by evidence from the text.

Structure

Activity 19 This activity asks students to think about the way that Noor has structured his plot.

Students may complete the table in the following way (there may be some variation on this – this is just an example which demonstrates how the story fits the structure):

	Explanation for 'Anil'
Opening	The reader is introduced to the setting in Malaysia. The difference from living in the UK is clear.
Development	We are introduced to Anil and his family.
Complication	Anil needs the toilet but he did not dare to go outside. The reader is told about the tree that eats children and the ghosts that he thinks might read his mind.
Climax	Anil hears voices and then discovers that the woman is being hanged. He confesses to what he has seen.
End	Anil is sent away to be educated. He is forced to leave his family and home against his will.

This activity is replicated on Worksheet 16d in the online resources.

Activity 20 This activity asks students to consider why Noor has used italics for some parts of the text.

The text in italics reveals Anil's most personal thoughts and gives his emotions at their most raw and painful. Noor wants to draw the reader's attention to these and so puts the text in italics.

Activity 21 This activity examines the ending of the story.

This requires a personal response from students but many may be left wondering what will become of Anil. He is forced to leave the village so abruptly and is so upset at being removed from his family that his bewildered and frightened frame of mind leaves the reader equally confused.

a   Students may want to know:

- where Anil is going and what will happen to him when he gets there
- whether his father will ever overcome the guilt and grief and forgive himself
- whether Marimathu is telling the truth.

b   Students may suggest that they feel unsettled at the end of the story because so many things appear to be left unresolved; worried and confused because Anil's future is uncertain; and sad because Anil and his father are so distraught. Whichever students select, ensure that they explain why they feel the way they do.

Outcomes

In this chapter students have learned how to:

- approach their analysis of 'Anil' by looking at the following elements: setting, point of view, character, theme and structure
- consider the context of 'Anil'
- think about the language and imagery the writer has used
- explore the meaning of the short story and consider the writer's intentions
- make a personal response to short stories.

17 Making your skills count in the exam: the Short Stories question

AO focus

AO1: Respond to texts critically and imaginatively; select and evaluate relevant textual detail to illustrate and support interpretation.

AO2: Explain how language, structure and form contribute to writers' presentation of ideas, themes and settings.

In this chapter your students will:

- learn about what is required of them in the exam for Unit 1, Section A: Exploring Modern Texts
- apply and practise their skills in order to respond to the exam question effectively.

About the exam

Structure and content of the exam

Questions on the Anthology short stories will be in Unit 1, Section A of the exam. Students must study one set text for Section A (Modern Prose or Drama) and one set text for Section B (Exploring Cultures) in this Unit. The seven short stories in the Anthology together comprise one of the available set texts for Section A. The paper will contain two questions on the short stories for both Foundation and Higher Tier. Students must answer one of these questions. Each question will have two parts (a) and (b). The Foundation questions will be more structured. One short story will be named and there will be a free choice of story, answering a question on the same theme, for part (b). It will not be a comparison question. It is recommended that students spend 45 minutes on Section A in the exam. There will be 30 marks available, making up 20 per cent of the total GCSE mark.

Candidates will be expected to consider:

- ideas, themes and issues
- characterisation
- settings.

All of these points must be underpinned by understanding the writers' use of language and technique.

How to prepare candidates for the exam

 Planning activity: 'On Seeing the 100% Perfect Girl One Beautiful Morning'

The examiners will be looking for:

Relevance: Candidates will need to read the question carefully and show how the stories link with the focus of the question.

Personal response: The examiners are looking for a personal relation to the two stories (there is no 'correct' answer).

Analysis: Candidates should show that they have engaged with the text and can provide detail to support their interpretations.

Exploration: Candidates should be able to offer an insightful response to the text and infer their own conclusions from it.

Communication: Candidates must make sure they communicate their ideas clearly and accurately.

Candidates will therefore need to:

- know the short stories really well and know the meanings of unfamiliar words
- be able to write confidently about setting, themes, characters and style
- learn linguistic terms so that they can use them to write confidently about how the author writes
- work through exam preparation and exam practice tasks.

It is also suggested that students should try writing answers to example questions, within the time allowed in the actual exam (45 minutes).

What students need to know

Candidates should:

- read the question carefully
- choose a question they fully understand and are confident about answering well
- underline the key words in the question, to help them to focus on answering it successfully
- follow any bullet points in the question
- make a plan
- integrate short quotations into their writing

- be aware of time. The 45 minutes should be divided equally between the two parts of the question

- allow themselves time to check their answers for sense and any errors of spelling and punctuation.

Introducing the questions

Below are some of the words found in different question types that candidates should be able to respond to:

- **Ideas** – refers to the story's themes.
- **An event** – something that happens in the story.
- **Your response** – what do you think the story is about? Comment on what you have learned about the content, setting, themes and style.
- **Your reaction** – how does the story make you feel when you read it? Comment on themes and style.
- **The methods used** – write about the words and stylistic features the writer has used.
- **The way things are described** – write about the words and stylistic features used to describe something, someone or somewhere in the story.
- **What the story is about** – write about the content and themes of the story.

Questions at Foundation Tier level will be more structured, with bullet points, for example:

a) Baines chooses to call her story 'Compass and Torch'.
Write about:
- why the compass and the torch are important in this story
- the ways Baines uses these objects to represent important ideas in the story.

b) Choose one other story where you think the title is effective.
Write about:
- what the title could mean
- how you think the title relates to the story.

(30 marks)

The equivalent Higher Tier question would be:

a) Write about the ways Baines uses the symbols of the compass and the torch to convey important ideas in 'Compass and Torch'.

b) Go on to write about the ways in which symbolism is used in one other story from the Anthology.

(30 marks)

For part a) of the question, a specific short story from the anthology will be named. For part b) the candidate will have a free choice. It is therefore important that students are confident of which other short story is suitable to use.

From the mark scheme the candidates should aim for the following:

Foundation Tier

For **quality of written communication** to achieve high marks the candidate should present relevant information coherently, employing structure and style to render meaning clear. The text produced should be legible. Spelling, punctuation and grammar should be sufficiently accurate.

For mid-range marks for **response to the texts** candidates should be able to demonstrate:

- a **considered/qualified** response to the task
- a **considered/qualified** response to the text
- details linked to interpretation
- **appreciation/consideration** of the writer's uses of language and/or form and/or structure and effect on readers/audience
- **thoughtful** consideration of ideas/themes/settings.

Higher Tier

For mid-range marks candidates should demonstrate:

- a **sustained** response to the task
- a **sustained** response to the text
- an **effective use** of details to support interpretation
- an **explanation** of effects of writer's uses of language and/or form and/or structure and effects on readers/audience
- **appropriate** comment on themes/ideas/settings.

For higher marks candidates should demonstrate:

- an **insightful exploratory** response to the task
- an **insightful exploratory** response to the text
- a **close analysis** of detail to support interpretation
- an **evaluation** of the writer's uses of language and/or/structure and/or form and effects on readers/audience
- a **convincing/imaginative** interpretation of ideas/themes/settings.

Practice exam questions

🔊 On your marks activity: 'Anil'

🔊 On your marks activity: 'Something Old, Something New'

Students are provided with sample exam questions for the both Higher and Foundation Tier in the Student Book.

Outcomes

In this chapter you have enabled students to:

- prepare for Section A of Unit 1 of the exam
- write a comprehensive response to the question set.